Saving The Test

by Mike Jakeman

www.ockleybooks.co.uk

Published by Ockley Books Ltd

First published 2013

ISBN 978-0-957141032

Front Cover designed by Michael Atkinson

Layout & design by Michael Kinlan

Printed & bound by:

Riley Dunn & Wilson Ltd.
Red Doles Lane
Huddersfield
West Yorkshire
HD2 1YE

For Ken

....

Contents

. . . .

Saving The Test
Foreword

by Jon Hotten

No-one forgets their first day of Test match cricket. I can even remember the date: Friday the 13th of August 1976, the summer that an endless heat-wave turned a green nation brown and had people queuing at standpipes in the streets. It was at Kennington Oval, the second morning of the Fifth Test between England and West Indies. There was a great sense of ritual to the day: lining up to click through the turnstile, buying a scorecard and a seat cushion, waiting for the five-minute bell to ring and the umpires to come down the pavilion steps, watching the fielding side walk out and then the batsmen, and hearing for the first time the strange silence made by many thousands of people saying nothing as the bowler runs in for the opening ball of the day...

To a kid like me it was huge and vivid, almost overpowering. Everything was bigger and faster and further, from the vastness of the outfield to the speed of the ball and how it was bowled, hit and thrown, and then the crowd, packed shoulder-to-shoulder on narrow wooden benches (hence the seat cushions—50p for the day and worth every penny) a powerful force in its own right.

Out in the middle was IVA Richards, 200 not out overnight and in the mood for more, getting ever closer to one of the great and apparently unapproachable records of the game: Garry Sobers' 365 not out, made against Pakistan almost 20 years before. Richards didn't just stroke the ball to boundary in the way it seemed on television. The movement that looked so languid when mediated by the cameras had a heft and a snap that could only be appreciated in the flesh. The ball rang from his bat with a sound I had never heard before, a bright crack with an echo of its own.

Richards got 291, bowled by Tony Greig just when it seemed that he might go past Sobers' mark. It was his final innings of 1976, a year in which he had made 1,710 Test runs—a record that would stand for another 30 years. Towards the end of the day, Clive Lloyd declared and Michael Holding came out and bowled at England's openers, Bob Woolmer and Dennis Amiss. He ran in from somewhere near the boundary at the speed of a 400-metre sprinter, the ball an indistinct fuzz as it flew from his hand.

That game was Test match number 781. As I write, the Ashes series is about to begin, and the first of those will be Test number 2090. There have been almost twice as many Test matches since

1976 as there were before it. That day, though, remains indelibly in my senses. It exists there as well as on paper and in the archives. That is the essence of Test cricket.

It is hard to think of a game that sits at greater odds with the speed of the times it is played in. It was created in an era of leisure, its durations designed to fill tours when men crossed the world by boat. It is almost entirely anachronistic and yet its rhythms, which are symphonic, still exert their deep pull. When Test cricket is good, it is unmatchably good, its inherent tensions ratcheted up by the days used in their creation. Many of the greatest Test matches of them all have been played in the last couple of decades.

The questions over its future have been asked almost since it started, but they have been answered so far by its constancy. That alone cannot make us complacent about its ability to survive. Nothing lasts forever, and Test cricket is subject to external, societal forces of commerce, time, and multimedia. As much as it is loved in some competing nations, others can be ambivalent to it. For every sold-out Ashes series, there is some dubious exercise in Dubai or Sharjah or at an empty Caribbean outpost constructed for a long-forgotten World Cup.

Test matches have co-existed peacefully with one-day internationals (ODIs) since 1971. Indeed, it is the poor old ODI that is looking more and more like a busted flush, its format exhausted by players who know it too well. The rise of Twenty20 cricket—the short form's heightened and logical conclusion—has not been as harmonious.

Whether the five-day game can withstand these forces are the questions that Mike Jakeman has set out to answer in this challenging and very necessary book. To me, the very fact that the book exists states the case for Test cricket: that someone would devote the time and energy and skill is still more evidence of what it does to you. Yet there are some deep enquiries here, and the answers are not always in view. It is recommended reading, and if you have picked it up and come this far, you probably already know why.

Jon Hotten, July 2013
Jon is the author of Muscle and The Years Of The Locust.
He writes the popular cricket blog, The Old Batsman.

Saving The Test
Introduction

> *"Test cricket has died a thousand deaths.*
> *But this time it might be serious."*
>
> *Peter Roebuck*

....

The idea for this book came to me at the end of the summer of 2011. More specifically, it arrived while I was standing in a carriage on the London Underground, reading the back pages of newspapers held aloft by other passengers. Earlier that afternoon England's Test cricketers had completed a 4-0 series win over those of India and the capital's sports journalists were triumphant. It was a victory so resounding that it sent England back to the top of the world rankings for the first time since 1980.

Although the newspapers celebrated with typical vigour, the mood among England supporters was more restrained. Watching footage of the moment that England won the series, when spinner Graeme Swann deceived India's impetuous number 11, Sri Sreesanth, into bottom-edging onto his stumps, it is noticeable that the crowd celebrated with a modest round of applause, rather than a jubilant roar. It was a clap to acknowledge that the team had played its part and done well. The reason for this, I believe, is that watching England play Test matches over the preceding two years had lulled supporters into a highly unusual state: a feeling of serenity.

In the 15 years that I have spent following cricket, watching England has gradually become a more enjoyable experience. In the late 1990s the prime attraction of an English summer was the masochistic joy of watching a new set of intimidating foreign bowlers making fools of our callow batsmen. Each summer brought a new reason to fear defeat. In 1997 I got my first look at Australia's Shane Warne and Glenn McGrath; in 1998, Allan Donald and Shaun Pollock of South Africa, and then Sri Lanka's Muttiah Muralitharan. The summer of 1999, which brought New Zealand to England, ought to have been different, but even the more modest pairing of Geoff Allott and Dion Nash proved devilish enough to condemn England to a series defeat.

Nevertheless, as a result of greater expenditure by the England and Wales Cricket Board (ECB)—enabled by selling broadcasting rights to Sky—a more coherent selection policy under the coach,

Duncan Fletcher, and a culture of professionalism introduced by the captain, Nasser Hussain, the subsequent decade saw a gradual improvement, punctuated by several notable victories. These included wins both in tricky places, such as Sri Lanka, and against manifestly superior opponents, such as Australia. However, when commentators come to analyse this period in depth, it will be the coming together of Andrew Strauss and Andy Flower as captain and coach in early 2009 that enabled England's transformation from a team that was less than the sum of its parts to one that became the best in the world.

Of the six nations that England played between the start of the summer of 2009 and the India series in 2011, only South Africa were able to hold them to a draw. The West Indies, Australia, Bangladesh, Pakistan and Sri Lanka were vanquished, albeit the last two in favourable conditions at home. There were a lot of victories in that time, 16 in 32 matches, which suggests that winning became a habit. The effect on the supporters was clear: they were becalmed. They were still coming through the gates with picnics in hand, but they expected to see England serve up a feast. Compare the aftermath of the India series with that of the glorious, madcap defeat of Australia in 2005. The earlier victory was celebrated with such wild euphoria because it was so totally unexpected. In the Strauss-Flower era, open-top bus rides and MBEs all round would have been unthinkable. The England team are no longer surprised by success. They insist upon it.

These impressions were cemented during the series with India, when England were able to extend their winning streak to 20 from 36 matches. Of those 20 wins, 10 were by an innings, which implies that, once England got the scent of victory, they did not let up. In the weeks before the First Test, the series was described as a yardstick by which England could measure themselves against the best. Despite England's good form, it was widely expected that India would demonstrate the skills that their hosts would need to imitate if they wished to supplant India at the top of the rankings. England had home advantage, but, in facing Rahul Dravid, Sachin Tendulkar, VVS Laxman and Virender Sehwag, they had to defeat one of the most experienced batting line-ups in Test history. At the start of the series, those four men had played a combined total of 550 Tests. England's XI, which was by no means inexperienced, had played a total of 502. The challenge that England faced was clear.

The first day of the series was a test of nerve. After 42 overs England were 107-2, scoring slowly and struggling to build momentum. Their tormentor-in-chief was the leader of the Indian bowling attack, Zaheer Khan, who had conceded just 18 runs from 13 testing overs. Aided by movement from the Lord's pitch, Zaheer was swinging the ball into and then away from the batsmen. Although no one quite realised it at the time, he was so integral to the success of the Indian team that the series was effectively over for the tourists as soon as he pulled his right hamstring three balls into the 43rd over. Without Zaheer, England sensed the fragility of the Indian bowling, and for four Tests played some wonderfully intense cricket. The English top-order batsman bullied the remaining, overworked Indian bowlers, playing with sufficient patience to leave good balls, while remaining alert enough to whip away the bad ones to the boundary.

Then, England's fast bowlers played with sufficient discipline to execute the team's strategy. They starved the Indian batsman of width, forcing the tourists to try to score off good-length balls, and then watched them perish when they grew impatient and tried to hit out. As the summer drew on, the crowd became more confident in England's ability, and, as a result, more relaxed. Even on the occasions when England appeared to be struggling—at 88-6 at Trent Bridge, or at 62-5 at Lord's, for example—they managed to wriggle out of danger, and put the pressure back on India. Curiously, England's batting seemed as vulnerable to collapse in 2011 as it did in the late 1990s, but, this time, the tail was capable of counter-attacking.

One of the truisms of sport is that fans are attracted to successful teams. Just as I found watching England's Tests more pleasurable in 2011 than I did in 1997, so did many others. The Oval was full to bursting for the Fourth Test, with capacity crowds of over 23,000 for all five days. Earlier in the summer, fans had queued outside the ticket booths at Lord's from 2am on the final day in the hope of getting a seat. By 10am the queue had swollen to 25,000. Some were there because the tickets were cheap (no-one at Lord's paid more than £20 for their seat on the fifth day), but most wanted to join in the celebratory atmosphere created by watching a winning team play to their potential.

After Lord's, when England had taken a 1-0 lead, but an Indian fight-back felt inevitable, it seemed as if cricket might transcend its minority appeal to define the sporting summer for the first time since 2005. But England's continued mastery over India meant that this was not to be the case. Instead, with the series' competitive edge blunted, attention shifted towards Tendulkar. At the age of 38, the Little Master needed to score just one more century to become the first man to score 100 international hundreds. For much of the series, England had his number. He scored just 34 and 12 at Lord's, 16 and 56 at Trent Bridge, and 1 and 40 at Edgbaston. Tendulkar received standing ovations whenever he walked on or off the field, but, as Vic Marks noted in *The Guardian*, "The time that elapses between [them] is reducing with every innings." In the first innings at The Oval he failed again, making 23 before being outwitted by Swann. In the second, however, it seemed that England were helping him on his way. They failed to appeal for a stumping when he had made 34, and then dropped him on 70 and 85. Yet, on 91, he inexplicably missed a straightforward flick to the leg side and the ball cannoned into his pad. Generous commentators suggested that he had been undone by a hint of reverse swing from Tim Bresnan, but, in reality, he simply made an error. When the umpire, Rod Tucker, raised his finger, The Oval gasped, as much in shock as in celebration.

Taken together, England's superlative display, the insatiable demand for tickets and the sub-plot of Sachin's bid for immortality suggest that 2011 was a vintage summer for Test cricket in England. Certainly, it was a big success for the cash-strapped counties, who were able to erect "sold-out" signs outside their grounds. Counties without a Test venue, such as Somerset and Northamptonshire, also benefited from extra revenue gleaned from holding tour matches for the Indians. Likewise, for Strauss and Flower, the summer of 2011 saw the realisation of a goal that must have seemed very distant after their first series together, which ended in defeat against a poor West Indies side. For Kevin Pietersen, who scored 202 in the First Test and 175 in the Fourth; for Dravid, who hit three centuries (which was three more than the rest of his team combined); and for Stuart Broad, who averaged 61 with the bat and 14 with the ball, there was personal satisfaction at a return to form or of expectations exceeded. But, for me, as I reflected on what the summer had taught me, I had doubts about the health of Test cricket.

Before I outline the thesis of this book, I would like to offer a counter-argument, one that suggests that Test cricket has never had it better. What began as a game between two nations in 1877 has become a global sport that has seen 2,000 matches played on four continents. Records, both team and individual, continue to be broken at a rapid pace, no matter how frequently commentators suggest that an achievement will prove insurmountable. At the end of 1997—the year in which I watched my first full series—the leading Test match wicket-taker was the Indian all-rounder Kapil Dev. With 434 victims, Dev was three ahead of New Zealand's Richard Hadlee, while only ten others had taken over 300. By the end of 2012, Dev had been relegated to sixth in the all-time list, behind Murali, Warne, Anil Kumble, McGrath, and another of England's tormentors from the 1990s, Courtney Walsh. The number of players with 300 wickets had doubled.

The same game can be played with batsmen, with similar results. At the end of 1997 Allan Border had scored more runs than anyone else, a total of 11,174, while seven others had scored over 8,000 Test runs. Sunil Gavaskar held the record for the highest number of centuries, with 34. By the end of 2012 Border was sixth. In his place stood Tendulkar, with 15,645 runs, and the former had also been supplanted by Ricky Ponting, Dravid, Jacques Kallis and Brian Lara. Membership of the 8,000 club had grown swiftly, to 24, and Tendulkar had added half as many again to Gavaskar's number of centuries.

Statistics, of course, tell only a fraction of the story. There are more runs scored and wickets taken than there used to be, because there is more Test cricket than ever. There were 198 Tests in the 1970s and 464 in the 2000s. (It might have been expected that the greater physical strain of playing more matches would have made careers shorter, but, in most cases, this has been offset by more sophisticated training methods and more diligent medical care.) Looking at averages, on the list of all-time batsmen with a minimum of 20 completed innings, none of the highest run-scorers listed above makes the top ten, although Kallis is just shy in 11th place. However, Tendulkar, Ponting, Dravid and Lara all make the top 30, along with seven other players who have also batted in the 21st century, meaning that the modern era is over-represented as a period in the history of Test matches.

The same cannot be said, however, for modern bowlers. The list of bowlers with the best average (having bowled in 20 innings) is dominated by those who plied their trade at the beginning of the 20th century, and is led by an English medium-pacer, George Lohmann, who took 112 wickets in 18 Tests at the mind-boggling average of 10.75. Only three men who have played in the current century make the top 30: the West Indies' Curtly Ambrose, Vernon Philander of South Africa and McGrath. There are several reasons for this, including the switch to covered pitches, and the more recent trend for flatter surfaces. Batting has also developed as a skill, which has inevitably left its mark on bowlers' figures. Again, statistics back this up: the average individual Test innings in the 1900s was 23.9 runs, compared with 32 in the 2000s. More matches and greater physical conditioning have enabled bowlers to take more wickets, but this has come at a greater cost.

But a wave of individual records is not enough by itself to argue that Test cricket is enjoying a golden age. What the modern game undoubtedly has over any other period in the past 30 years is greater competition at the top end. Only once between the late 1970s and the late 2000s did the baton held by the best team in the world pass from one cricket team to another. That moment occurred in May 1995, when the West Indies, who were on an unbeaten streak of 29 Test series dating back to 1980, were defeated 2-1 at home by Mark Taylor's emerging Australians. It had been more than two decades since the Windies had lost a series in the Caribbean. During that period they rolled out their legendary fast bowlers with the efficiency of cars on a production line. That was until they encountered Steve Waugh.

After beginning his Test career as a bowling all-rounder, Waugh reinvented himself as a batsman in an attempt to secure his place in the team. Such transformations are rare, particular those involving such a dramatic change of temperament. When batting down the order, he played with freedom and panache, but he aspired to become the backbone of the team. In the Fourth Test, with the series balanced at 1-1, Waugh came to the crease to join his twin brother, Mark, with Australia struggling at 73-3 in reply to the Windies' 265. The ball had dominated the bat for the entire series, and no batsman had been able to play a decisive innings. However, the Waughs managed to grind down Walsh and Ambrose, and, by the time that Mark was out for 126, Australia had a lead of 39. Steve batted expertly with the tail before he was eventually the last man out, for exactly 200. It was his first Test double-hundred. Having demoralised the Windies in the field, Warne and Paul Reiffel ran through them for 213 to give Australia a thumping win. Waugh would go on to inherit the captaincy from Taylor and stamp not only his own gritty character onto the team, but, more importantly, the opposition into the turf. *Wisden* noted that, of the 425 balls he faced when making his 200, more than 150 were short-pitched, yet not once did he attempt the hook shot, as he thought it too risky. Instead, he blocked, ducked and, when he could do neither, wore the short deliveries, as he did six times in the innings. Rarely has a batsman put such a high price on his wicket.

Such durability would be a feature of the great Australian sides that were to follow Waugh's war in the Caribbean. They were unable to match the invincibility of the Windies (they had a knack of losing series in India), but, in between tours to the sub-continent, they set a record of 16 consecutive Test wins. The first came in Harare against Zimbabwe in October 1999 and the last in Mumbai in February 2001. Then, against South Africa in December 2005, they set off on another spree, winning another 16 in a row, until defeat against India in 2008.

However, just as the West Indies eventually stumbled, so too did Australia. In 2008 Australia's win in the Caribbean was emulated by South Africa's success down under. The heroic role played by Steve Waugh was replicated by the South African captain, Graeme Smith. Smith was not expected to play in the series because of an elbow injury. Instead, he delayed surgery and had his own blood injected into a tear in the muscle to sustain himself. He shrugged off the pain to score 326 runs in the three Tests at an average of 65.2, and ended the last game batting at 11, after his hand was broken earlier in the innings. Such is his competitive streak that he came out to bat, broken hand and all, despite the fact that South Africa had already clinched the series. His motivation was that South Africa would have supplanted Australia at the top of the world rankings if they batted out a draw. As so often, cricket proved a cruel game: Smith was out for three and Australia remained, at least according to the rankings, the best team in the world. For only the second time in 30 years, there was room at the top. But for whom?

In the past four years, the mantle of the best team in the world has been passed around between South Africa, India, and England, giving the sport a sense of competition that had been lacking in the previous three decades. This is not a universally held view; Gideon Haigh likens South Africa's ascent to the top after Australia's defeat to England in the 2009 Ashes to "a bureaucrat being promoted because of the incompetence of his predecessor". This is uncharitable, as South Africa had demonstrated their effectiveness by beating Australia only six months before. Haigh then gazes into his navel, mournfully suggesting that the crumbling of the Australian team "ended not just a dynasty, but the last such dynasty and perhaps the whole idea of dynasties itself". The Australians of the early 21st century were a great team—possibly the best team of them all—but they were not so great that there can never be another as good. The lifeblood of sport is, to borrow another of Haigh's phrases, "the tang of competition". Such a tang should be celebrated, not resented. And now, between the top four teams at least, Test cricket has it.

To demonstrate this, take a few minutes and write down your best current Test XI. This should be a team that can perform all round the world, equally comfortable on greentops, dustbowls and featherbeds. Its batsmen should be able patiently to endure high-quality bowling and mercilessly shred a wayward attack. Its bowlers must have the control to generate pressure and the aggression to intimidate batsmen. My team is at the end of this introduction. I suspect that your team includes players from at least four Test-playing nations. Mine has five, and it would be more if either of India's future stars, Cheteshwar Pujara or Virat Kohli, had demonstrated their excellence in just a few more matches. But the point is that, for a few years at least, we should be in an age of open and exciting Test cricket.

Between September 2011 and August 2016 the top five Test teams (at the beginning of that period)—England, South Africa, India, Australia and Sri Lanka—will play each other home and away, with each hoping to develop the kind of dominance enjoyed by the Windies of the 1980s and the Australians of the 1990s. It should be a glorious time to be a cricket fan. However, the central argument of this book is that the environment in which Test cricket is played, if not the sport itself, is not in a fit state to thrive.

It is common affliction among those that take cricket to their hearts to depict the game as lurching from one crisis to the next. As long ago as 1939 Sir Donald Bradman denounced in *Wisden* "the quickening of modern tempo, the more Americanised trend, which is demanding speed, action and entertainment value" that "behoves all of us to realise we are the custodians of the welfare of cricket and must guard its future even more zealously than its present". The number of contemporary cricket journalists who have not described an emerging story as "the biggest crisis since Packer" must be very small indeed.

Yet the crisis described in *Saving the Test* is not the sort posed by singular threats, such as an ambitious media heavyweight with too little respect for tradition, or networks of illegal bookmakers bribing players to throw matches. It is a crisis generated by a number of different pressures, which, when taken together, work against the kind of thrilling, combative, nerve-jangling and downright epic sport that Test match cricket at its best provides. The sport still works, but the environment in which it is set is ailing. Test match cricket is trying to survive in a time of administrative weakness within its governing body, self-interested politicking among the national boards and easy fame and fortune for mediocre players. It has to compete within a cricket calendar that has been stuffed to the gills, robbing players and fans of any sense of anticipation and the timing of fixtures of any coherence. It has to offer the supreme test of skill when the financial rewards to its players are firmly tilted towards the hit-and-giggle cricket of Twenty20 (T20). It has to offer consistency and clarity when there is no consensus on the extent to which technology can be used in the game. It has to draw in the crowds when groundsmen are pressured to prepare pitches that drain the life out of a match in order that five days worth of tickets can be sold. It has to rid itself of corruption at a time when sensational reporting is the only way to sell newspapers. And it has to remain competitive at a time when income from broadcasting rights is hugely uneven. Test cricket is not yet broken, but it is being made to carry a heavy burden.

The effects of this burden on the cricket itself were brought into focus during the 2011 England-India series. Most obviously, England ran out as victors against a team that had become a victim of the calendar. MS Dhoni's Indians were both undercooked and exhausted by the time that they arrived for a long series in England, owing to an incoherent and frenetic schedule that encompassed the Indian Premier League (IPL), a World Cup and a Test series against the

West Indies in the four months before they washed up in England.

The increase in the number of matches is a direct consequence of the popularity of T20 cricket. T20 matches—and the IPL in particular—now generate so much of the sport's revenue that they have to be squeezed into the calendar, whatever the cost. T20 has brought a new wave of innovation and a greater sense of urgency to Test cricket, as well as further opening up cricket's labour market. But there is also a big risk that playing three forms of the game simultaneously will demand too much from players, especially those that are still learning the game. For the next generation of young players to scale the heights of their predecessors, more has to be done to nurture their development.

The England-India series was also notable for the refusal of the Board of Control for Cricket in India (BCCI) to sanction the use of the Hawk-Eye ball-tracking system. Although this has created the unhappy situation where some Tests are officiated using the Decision Review System (DRS) and some are not, the use of technology in cricket is a much wider, and more important, argument. The use of the DRS has changed Test cricket forever, but not necessarily in ways that the authorities intended. It also has big implications for the future of umpires, who are losing their previously unshakeable authority.

Another endangered species in Test cricket is the bouncy pitch. The last decade saw a series of soporific, slow, low surfaces that generate huge scores, few wickets, and many, many draws. In order to protect their gate receipts and appease broadcasters, Test match hosts have become more encouraging than ever of pitches that will guarantee five days of play. However, even if flat surfaces result in higher revenue in the short term, the long-term effect on the sport will be detrimental, if the balance between bat and ball is lost.

Thankfully, the England-India series appeared to escape the malignancy of match-fixing, but the Lord's Test of 2010 between England and Pakistan showed that cricket, like cycling and athletics, has yet to resolve its vulnerability to corruption. However, much of what was written about the "spot-fixing" scandal has been misleading or inaccurate. There is a big difference between what we think we know about fixing and what has actually been proven. Nevertheless, given the intertwined history of cricket and corruption, we can be sure that another scandal of some sort is just around the corner.

Finally, in the time since Kerry Packer initiated a wave of deregulation in broadcasting markets, cricket has been transformed from a game reliant on gate receipts to one in thrall to television. It has become many times richer, but also many times more unequal. The consequence is that Test match cricket has become a sport in which only four or five teams are consistent, with the rest no more than fodder for the rich. It desperately needs to become more competitive.

Saving the Test examines each of these pressures. But first, a disclaimer. Running through this book will be the relationship between Test and limited-overs cricket. I see this bond as a form of sibling rivalry. Tests, ODIs and T20s compete for attention from players, administrators, broadcasters and fans in the manner of brothers and sisters, and each requires that attention to thrive. Like any bunch of siblings, each has its relative strengths and weaknesses. Even to its greatest advocate, there are days of Test cricket that seem to stretch out into eternity. Watching two well-set batsmen on a slow pitch can see the mind wander, legs cramp and the bar call. T20 cricket, in England at least, embraces the drinking culture: many domestic games are scheduled for Thursday and Friday nights to pull in the beery after-work crowds. But organisers also seem curiously distrustful of allowing the cricket to entertain. Instead, T20 is lumbered with unnecessary and cringe-inducing fripperies, such as dancing girls and live music. When batsmen are going at ten runs an over, there is no need for additional fireworks. Sat uncomfortably between these two extremes is one-day cricket, a classic middle sibling. On a bad day, ODIs can fail to offer either a high-quality examination of technique or the visceral thrill of seeing the ball disappear to all parts of the ground. Any single-innings game is also reliant on both teams getting off to a decent start, or the match quickly subsides.

Let me be clear: this book is not advocating *siblicide*. If there were only room for a single form of cricket, I am in no doubt that Test matches should prevail, but those that insist blindly that T20 or ODIs should be put down are as blinkered as those that say Test cricket is an anachronism. Unlike Duncan Hamilton, I can swallow "the razzmatazz: the show-off announcers who yell about what has just happened or what is to come... the act of forced jollity, like someone at a party constantly blowing a streamer in your face and telling you to enjoy yourself... the coloured clothing and the white ball that always ends up looking grubby... the asinine suffix monikers attached to each country... the weary, tedious soundtrack accompanying every boundary or wicket". I am willing to put up with these gimmicks—which are already tired and detracting from the action—because I accept the reality that Test cricket is a minority sport. It can be infernally complicated. The action is sporadic; expert technique is not always easy to spot. But, if a few thousand spectators drawn to the easy thrills and spills of T20 spot something interesting, and that interest leads them to Lord's on the day of a Test match, then I think that T20 will have earned its keep.

That and the fact that it is demonstrably wrong to consider ODIs and T20 as the illegitimate, younger siblings of the one true son. Cricket has been played in more forms that you or I could fathom. It has been played as an individual, single-wicket game, and internationals have been played between teams of two, eight, eleven and most numbers in the teens. It has been played indoors and out; innings have been as short as five overs and as long as the length of time that the boat can be docked in the port. When all of these variations are considered, it is striking that we have been left with Test cricket, and the two forms that look most like it. There is Test cricket, and there are the games that try to condense it into a single day of play.

But the clarity of a guaranteed result does not outweigh the main reason why Test matches represent the best of cricket. Tests are best precisely because they are expansive. The five-day format permits, nay, encourages, the greatest feats. Two famous not-out innings in Johannesburg bear this out. The first is Ricky Ponting's 140 in the 2003 World Cup Final. Never the biggest hitter and always a reluctant slogger, Ponting nonetheless used just 121 balls to power Australia to an insurmountable total against Sourav Ganguly's Indians. Rarely has a batsman seen the ball more clearly or hit it more cleanly. But how much further could he have gone? We will never know. He could have gone on for two days and made 500, or whirled himself into a frenzy and been out within an over. He wrung every last run from his innings, but he remained constrained by the rules of the game, which allowed him only 121 balls. It was one of the best limited-overs innings of all time. But that word "limited" is key.

The second innings is Michael Atherton's 185 not out against

South Africa in the 1995/96 Test series. By all logic, England should have lost the match comprehensively: in theory they needed 479 to win, but, more pertinently, when Atherton walked out to bat, the Test was only at its half-way point. The rest of the match stretched out in front of him, all the way to the horizon. That he remained steadfast at the crease for almost 11 hours and faced nearly 500 balls is now part of cricketing legend. In his autobiography he describes how "For the only time in my career I was in the zone... It was a state of both inertia and intense concentration and *I knew* that I was in total control and they couldn't get me out". Doubtless, Ponting was in a similar sort of zone, but the limited-overs format meant that he remained in it only for a little over two hours. The Test match offered Atherton no such escape. Or, perhaps more accurately, its greater duration gave him a bigger opportunity to show his talent. And, like the very best players, he took it.

The demands that the expansiveness of Test cricket puts on players is mirrored in what it asks of its spectators. The number of supporters with lifestyles that allow them the luxury of watching all five days of a Test is very small indeed, so most spectators are asked to assimilate themselves into a game that may be just beginning, be about to end or be somewhere in the middle. When sitting down to watch the second day of a Test with the team batting first resuming on 260-5, it is not immediately obvious to anyone who is on top. It is not the same as a half-time score of 2-0 or 21-7, or 6-3, 4-2. The value of those 250 runs depends on the weather, the state of the pitch, the length of the tail and the quality of the bowling. Those five wickets might have been scant reward for some superb bowling or thrown away through loose shots. The only way to discover whether the team with the 250 runs or that with the five wickets is in the ascendant is to immerse yourself in the match; to watch the body language of the fielders, the confidence of the batsmen in hitting their shots, the exhortations of the fielding captain as he shuffles his bowlers.

If Test cricket relied upon the adrenaline of a 25-yard volley finding the back of the net or a cross-court forehand winner, then it would have died many decades ago. The pleasure of the Test is a slower, less immediate sort. It is of watching the match ebb and flow as each team tries to take it out of the reach of the other. It is of watching batsmen fighting their instinct to attack in the face of probing bowling;

of bowlers measuring out their delivery stride to ensure that their run-up to the crease is smooth; of fielders furiously shining the ball in an attempt to make it swing; of the sweep of an umpire's arm as he signals a four; of the sun breaking through the clouds for the first time in the day. To achieve an expert understanding of Test cricket, of its many permutations and consequences, to gauge which team is on top and pick the player with the skill to succeed, take a lifetime. For all these reasons it is, undoubtedly, a game worth saving.

Best Test XI:

Smith (C)
Cook
Amla
Sangakkara
Clarke
de Villiers
Prior (W)
Philander
Steyn
Ajmal
Anderson
12th man: Swann

Chapter One
The Tour

> *"I go on holiday for longer*
> *than that series is going to last."*
>
> Dale Steyn
>
> . . . .

In April 1972 the Australians arrived in a wet and chilly England to contest the summer's Ashes series. It was a young team, but one that was eager to avenge a harrowing home defeat to England in 1970/71. It was also a team under new leadership. The established captain, Bill Lawry, was gone, having been ignominiously sacked before the final (and decisive) Test of the preceding Ashes, an event that divided the Australian cricket community. His replacement, Ian Chappell, was touring England for the first time, as were nine of the other 16 members of his squad. The tourists' inexperience meant that England were strong favourites for the series.

However, the matches that followed were more competitive and entertaining than most had expected. England won the First Test at Old Trafford comfortably, but were dismantled in the second by a 25-year-old swing bowler playing in his first ever Test match. Bob Massie did little more than bowl a consistent length, but, with the help of some late swing, took a scarcely credible 16 wickets in the match, and, in doing so, wrote himself into cricket history.[1] After a draw in Nottingham that kept the series at 1-1, England beat Australia in less than three days on a questionable pitch at Headingley that took spin from the first afternoon. The win meant that England retained the Ashes, but ten wickets for the emerging Dennis Lillee at The Oval ensured that Australia pulled off a very respectable 2-2 draw in the series.

The tourists may have been inexperienced, but they were also well prepared. The reason that they were able to contribute to what the distinguished Australian commentator Richie Benaud described as "the best series I have had the pleasure of seeing since retiring as a player", was their schedule. When the Australian opener, Keith Stackpole, strode out to bat on the first morning of the series on

---

1   *No Test bowler had ever taken so many wickets on his debut. Massie's name was written out of the record books in 1988 when Narendra Hirwani took the same number of wickets, but for one run fewer.*

June 8th, he had already spent almost eight weeks in England. He was fit, acclimatised and well practised. The first innings at Old Trafford was his 11th of the tour, and he had played at four of the five Test match grounds.

Stackpole was one of the many in the Australian team that were touring England for the first time, but he arrived in the country in good touch, having scored a century and two fifties in his previous four Test innings, against a World XI in Australia. He had also averaged over 50 against England in the 1970/71 Ashes. A big and solidly built man, Stackpole exploited his physical attributes to play in an aggressive and uncompromising manner that was at odds with the style of the age. He only really knew one way to play, which was to combat hostile, short-pitched bowling with vigorous hooks and pulls. His refusal to alter his approach meant that he did enough to keep the fielders at square and fine leg interested, but the weight of runs that he scored also indicates that he was judicious in his shot selection.

Compared with other distinguished openers of his day, such as Lawry, or England's Geoffrey Boycott, he was a bit of an oddity; a man who took risks when conservatism was in fashion. He was also a victim of an unspoken piece of cricketing prejudice, which says that aggressive players are somehow more indebted to luck than those who grind out their runs. It is also assumed that players willing to go after the ball do not value their wickets as highly, and are therefore less committed to the team. Stackpole's reputation has been sullied by this criticism, and, as a result, he is best remembered for an infamous reprieve in the First Test of the 1970/71 Ashes. Having scored just 18, he was seemingly short of his ground when Boycott threw down the stumps. The umpire was convinced that Stackpole had made his ground and allowed him to bat on, which he did, to make the only double century of his Test career. Although he subsequently played with freedom and skill, the innings was perceived to have been devalued by the let-off. This stigma means that he is missing from the top, or even the second tier of Australian Test openers. But between 1970 and 1973, he was indispensible at the top of the Australian order, an imposing presence and a reliable plunderer of runs.

There were few runs to be made in the soggy warm-up matches for the 1972 Ashes. Stackpole made 18 before being bowled by a young Tony Greig in the first game at Arundel, a 50-over match against a scratch team assembled by the Duke of Norfolk, which Australia lost by 28 runs. The traditional game against Worcestershire at New Road—made famous by Sir Donald Bradman, who hit four double hundreds and a century in five innings at the ground—was ruined by rain, although Stackpole still managed to get out twice without passing 50. The weather also intervened in matches against Lancashire and Nottinghamshire, before two single-figure scores against Surrey rounded off a wretched month. His fortunes changed in mid-May, when he hit an unbeaten 119 in a 9-wicket win for the tourists against a strong Hampshire team, featuring Barry Richards and Gordon Greenidge. There was little joy for Stackpole, however, in the remaining games against the Marylebone Cricket Club (MCC), Glamorgan and then Derbyshire, much of which was again lost to rain. Nevertheless, by the time that the First Test rolled around, Stackpole was able to show the benefit of weeks of match practice.

Having seen England grind their way to a first-innings score of 249 on a lively pitch that offered Lillee and his new-ball partner, David Colley, more assistance than they were able to exploit, Stackpole and debutant, Bruce Francis, began the Australian reply. The first over was bowled by England's premier fast bowler, John Snow, the self-styled "cricket rebel", who had taken 31 wickets at an average of 22.8 against Lawry's Australians in the 1970/71 series. His tour ended prematurely after he broke his finger on a boundary fence attempting to catch a six hit by Stackpole in the final Test in Sydney. Perhaps with their previous encounter in mind, and aware of Snow's notoriously short temper, Stackpole decided to take the fight to the bowler, hooking the first ball of the innings to the boundary. Snow's partner, Geoff Arnold, proved to be a tougher prospect to get away, but Stackpole still scored freely, despite Francis falling lbw to Basil D'Oliveira for 27. Moments later, the skipper, Ian Chappell, went for a golden duck. Greg Chappell offered a bit more resistance, making 24 and allowing Stackpole to accelerate to a rapid 53 from 85 balls, before being trapped lbw by Arnold. Thereafter, the Australians slid to 142 all out, with Arnold and Snow sharing eight wickets.

In England's second innings Greig made his second fifty of the match in a total of 234, to set Australia a difficult total of 342 to win.

Despite more slipshod batting at the other hand, Stackpole remained resolute, hitting six fours in a score of 67 before he was bowled, just as he had been at Arundel, by Greig. Some late-order pyrotechnics from Rod Marsh lifted the Australian score to the respectability of 252, but they were still defeated by 89 runs.

Stackpole's promising form at Old Trafford continued throughout the series. He made an unbeaten 57 in the win at Lord's, a century at Nottingham, 52 at Headingley and 79 in the final Test at the Oval. This meant he ended the series with 485 runs, the highest individual total on either team, and an average of 53.9. It was a performance good enough to ensure that he joined Lillee as one of *Wisden's* five Cricketers of the Year. The *Almanack* described how "There were some, the England players included, who believed that by the time the 1972 Test series was over Stackpole was batting with a magic wand rather than an ordinary sliver of willow." However, his reputation as a fortunate player was inescapable: "Every so often he managed to get an outside edge to an attempted cut or drive and, in more cases than not, the ball flew clear of the field. Some of the opposition regarded this as lucky..."

I never had the pleasure of watching Stackpole bat in person, but, even at a distance, I feel that this is tosh. When a batsman is confident in his form, attuned to the pitch and has had a look at the bowlers, judgment takes over and he is able to decide which of the deliveries outside of off-stump can be safely edged down to third man, and which need to be blocked or left alone. Of course, this judgment can be fallible—Stackpole was dropped twice in the second over of the first innings at Old Trafford—but to suggest that the performance of a batsman who has scored almost 500 runs in a series is built on luck is to denigrate the art of batting itself.

Stackpole's runs were built on his ability, but this was cultivated by the careful planning of the Australian administrators, who understood the necessity of allowing their players to acclimatise to an unfamiliar setting. It is rare for the ball to move as much off the seam in Melbourne as it can do at Lord's, while even Sydney, which, among Australian pitches, traditionally offers the most help to the spinners, does not turn as much as Old Trafford. Faced with the difficulty of an inexperienced team and a new set of conditions to master, the Australian Board of Control for International Cricket (nowadays known more concisely as Cricket Australia or CA), made the decision to schedule a long build-up to the Test series, with 12 practice matches against English teams. This was vindicated by the fact that the Australians were more competitive than was expected. When reflecting on the series, the Australian wicketkeeper, Rod Marsh, suggested it was only the unusual pitch at Headingley that prevented the tourists from regaining the Ashes. In the week before the match, heavy rain saturated the square, preventing the use of the heavy roller. The surface also fell victim to *fusarium* disease, which "made the pitch turn square". Marsh believed that the outbreak was convenient, as it "suited England a hell of a lot more than it suited us." His dark mutterings, to the effect that the Yorkshire groundsman had participated in some sort of fungal skulduggery, were dismissed by the Test and County Cricket Board's (TCCB) Pitches Committee. Nevertheless, Stackpole described the Saturday of the Headingley Test as "easily the most depressing night of my life". He was furious at the fact that the tourists had been undone by precisely what they had worked the hardest to overcome: the unfamiliar playing conditions.

In the 40 years since the 1972 Ashes, the type of rigorous match practice enjoyed by the Australians has largely disappeared. Warm-up or practice matches are considered a luxury, to be indulged in only if the international calendar allows. The money that now flows into the sport through lucrative broadcasting deals, combined with the expansion of domestic and international limited-overs competitions, means that the fixture list is being tightly squeezed. Time spent in the nets or playing local sides is now seen as expensive—there is no money in screening practice games against invitational XIs. Instead, weary players are shuttled from tour to tour, just about able to remember which form of cricket is coming up next. At the start of an overseas tour you might see a loose two or three-day game played by two teams of 12 or 13-a-side, but it will not be enough to prevent the visitors from being thrust into a Test or one-day series unprepared.

This compression of the calendar is having an adverse effect on Test cricket. The proliferation of short tours, accompanied by inadequate time to train and practise, prevents players from adapting to new surroundings. A lack of recovery time between tournaments, and, increasingly, between Tests in a series, also increases the risk of players breaking down injured. Short tours impede the development of rivalries, while back-to-back Tests deny captains and coaches the time to generate new tactics and plans. This trend is not a new development. The pressure on the length of tours increases each time that the sport's governing body, the International Cricket Council (ICC), introduces a new tournament to the calendar or when an interloper steals a few weeks for itself, such as the Indian Premier League (IPL). But the effects on Test cricket became irrefutable during India's visit to England in 2011. What should have been a gripping, summer-long spectacle was notable not for its technical skill, but for its frequent displays of ineptitude. The nadir was reached in the Third Test, when, needing a win to keep the series alive, the Indian selectors chose to bring their explosive opening batsman, Virender Sehwag, back into the team after he missed the first two games through injury. The varying experiences of Stackpole and Sehwag illustrate the difficulties facing Test cricket.

At the peak of his career, Sehwag was a phenomenon. His style would transform Test match batting forever, if only it could be imitated. Instead, he is likely to be remembered as a glorious eccentric, who defied easy comparison and made a mockery of convention. He does this by playing simply the most aggressive cricket ever seen. Occasionally in a Test match a batsman will be beaten by a *jaffa*, a ball that is too quick and moves too much for the batsman to edge—too good, in other words, even to get the batsman out. The batsman will often meet the bowler's eye and smile ruefully in recognition of the quality of the ball. But you will never see Virender Sehwag do this, not because he is lacking in humour, but because he does not believe that a ball can be too good to hit. Rather, every delivery is a potential boundary, if only the batsman is quick enough.

He does not have the classical technique that pleases coaches, but he has found an unorthodox method that works. His head stays absolutely still as the ball is bowled, eyes fixed on picking the length of the ball as it travels towards him. Unlike many aggressive, modern batsmen—Kevin Pietersen, for instance—he does not look to get a big stride in towards the ball. Rather, he waits, with relatively little footwork, which enables him to swing his arms through in a perfect arc as the ball arrives. It is a very economical technique, which he seems to have arrived at by stripping away unnecessary detail. Because he makes relatively few adjustments to his stance, he is able to focus so closely on the ball as it moves, and to get his hands, as quick as a magician's, into the right position to meet the ball cleanly and send it rocketing to the boundary. Like many South Asian batsman, he has been described as being uncomfortable against short-pitched bowling, but his relatively short stature makes this less of a problem, as he is able quickly to get into position to hook.

Allied to, or perhaps resulting from, Sehwag's uncomplicated technique is the gift of extraordinary focus. Like his former team-mate, Rahul Dravid, or England's Alastair Cook, he is capable of clearing his mind of distractions in order better to perform the same task over and over again—although, in his case, it is not to leave the ball outside off stump, but to smack it for four. It is his aggressive attitude and simple technique that has enabled him to become a statistical freak. In the Twenty20 (T20) era, the sight of a batsman coming to the crease, whirling and thrashing like a typhoon for five or six overs, and then blowing himself out, is a familiar one. Sehwag rarely does this; he marries occupation of the crease with wreaking havoc. This has enabled him to post eight Test scores over 150, four double centuries and two triple centuries. Nor does he discriminate against good bowlers. He scored a nonsensical 319 off 304 balls against South Africa in 2008, against an attack that featured Dale Steyn, Makhaya Ntini and Morne Morkel. He also hit a double century against Muttiah Muralitharan's Sri Lanka on Murali's home ground. And this is to disregard other crucial innings, such as an 83 off 68 balls against England in 2008, which set the tone for a successful fourth-innings chase of a supposedly ungettable 387.

Early in Sehwag's career, the cricket press struggled to define him, falling back on the sobriquet "chancy" as if this were somehow synonymous with his natural aggression. In 2004, months after he made his first triple century—309 against Pakistan in Multan—he scored 155 against Australia in Chennai. The editor of *Wisden India*, Dileep Premachandran, described his innings as "a mix of glorious strokeplay, wild heaves and impetuous hoicks" and compared it unflatteringly to another innings of 155 against Australia by Sachin Tendulkar in 1998. Sehwag is no more of a lucky player than Dravid, but, just like Stackpole, the fact that he hits the ball in the air is, for some, enough to indicate that he is reliant on the gods for his success.

Again, this is nonsense. The bottom line is that he scores more runs than most, and he gets them at a faster rate than anyone in history.

But, for all of his undoubted talent, Sehwag should not have played against England in the Third Test in 2011. In the first over of the match, his opening partner, Gautam Gambhir, took two fours off the bowling of James Anderson. Sehwag then faced Stuart Broad. The bowler's first ball was just short of a length and, Sehwag, with his characteristically high back-lift, initially aimed to cut it through the off side. However, as the ball moved in the air, he realised that it wasn't wide enough to hit cleanly. Instead, Sehwag pulled his body away from the ball, but, because his feet were rooted to the spot, couldn't move his hands out of the way fast enough. The ball kissed the top of his glove and sailed through to the wicketkeeper. Although Broad's delivery was tricky, Sehwag was rusty. His lack of practice in English conditions, where the ball can bounce unpredictably, was exposed. But worse was to follow.

After India were skittled for 224, England, led by Cook with 294, piled on an extraordinary 710-7. This left India needing 486 runs just to make England bat again. A solid first-innings partnership was crucial to their reply. Gambhir faced the first ball and drove it firmly down to extra cover for three. That put Sehwag on strike to face Anderson, the spearhead of the England attack, for the first time in the series. Anderson's next ball was a bit short, and he found a touch of away swing. But the length and movement of the ball were irrelevant. Sehwag had decided that he was going to drive it before it had even left the bowler's hand. Because the ball pitched outside off stump and was moving away, his firm push edged the ball into the waiting hands of Andrew Strauss, for a simple catch at first slip. Sehwag was out again, and for a king pair.

Unluckily for him, he had become the 13th man in the history of Test cricket to make a king pair, and, give or take Adam Gilchrist, probably the most famous. But the moment had a wider significance, beyond adding to Sehwag's burgeoning collection of unlikely statistics and records. His short stay at the crease demonstrated the inappro-priateness of his being on the field at all. One part of his game—his attacking intent— was present, but his mind was somewhere else. In the first innings he was unable to react to Broad's extra bounce and, in the second, he failed to respond to Anderson's away-swing. It was the worst of all outcomes for the Indian administrators: not only did their man fail in both innings, but he did so in such spectacular fashion that it shone a light on their flawed selection policy and, by extension, their management of the tour.

Sehwag went into the Third Test having played just a single innings on the tour—a practice match against Northamptonshire, in which he made 8 from 25 balls, before he was out lbw to a bowler who usually played for the county's second XI. Prior to that, he had not played any cricket for four months, as he was recovering from shoulder surgery. He had not played a Test match since the turn of the year. It is easy to imagine the selectors' dilemma prior to Edgbaston: India were 2-0 down and needed a win to keep the series alive. Sehwag's deputy, a promising but callow batsman, Abhinav Mukund, had made just 64 runs in four innings in the series. There was little point, they would have thought, in holding Sehwag back until the Fourth Test, when not even another of his triple centuries would have rescued the series. Summing up the selectors' gamble, *The Guardian*'s Vic Marks wrote:

"[Sehwag] has no right to be in any sort of form to produce an epic Test innings, but for a batsman like him it sometimes takes just one shot. It might be an effortless, perfectly timed cover drive, probably with only an imperceptible movement of the feet, which gets the juices flowing again. After that, anything is possible."

Sehwag's career has been about making the unlikely seem routine, but not even he could conjure a meaningful innings when neither physically nor mentally fit to play. The story behind Sehwag's selection gets murkier the deeper one digs. He first suffered shoulder problems while playing in the IPL in 2008. During the same tournament in 2009 he aggravated his shoulder and was forced to have surgery. It is not known whether it was recommended that he cut down his schedule to reduce the chance of the injury recurring a second time, but it has been suggested that he was in pain again before the World Cup in April 2011. However, this did not prevent him from playing in eight of India's nine matches in that victorious campaign or from captaining the Delhi Daredevils in the IPL, which began just six days later. After 11 IPL matches (in which he scored over 400 runs), Sehwag admitted defeat and had another operation on his shoulder, which ruled him out of India's tour to the West Indies and the first two Tests in England.

The unavoidable conclusion to draw from this saga is that Sehwag and the governing body of Indian cricket, the Board of Control for Cricket in India (BCCI), saw the Tests in England and the West Indies as inconsequential. For fans of Test cricket this is a bitter pill. But the way that the cricket calendar is scheduled is such that it is also difficult to find fault in Sehwag's judgment. Not even the biggest advocate of five-day cricket could demand that he forsake the chance to compete, and win, the World Cup in his home country.

And such are the sums on offer to players in the IPL that financial security can be assured for less than two months of work. Even for those less enamoured of T20, who see the signing of an IPL contract as a Mephistophelian pact, it cannot be denied that the old devil offers a pretty tempting deal. Sehwag is not the kind of player for whom the IPL makes the biggest difference—he is a superstar playing in the sport's most lucrative country. Its main beneficiaries are the journeymen pros who are towards the end of their careers and have not played international cricket, and those from the West Indies, Pakistan or Bangladesh, whose IPL wages dwarf the remuneration that they receive from playing Tests or one-day internationals (ODIs). But that does not mean that Sehwag is immune to the promise of an enormous wage for a six-week thrash.

The biggest problem is not the choices made by the players. The ease with which Kerry Packer was able to sign up cricketers for his breakaway World Series Cricket in 1977 showed that most will follow the cash. The problem is that the players have to make a choice at all. This was the first of many mistakes by the BCCI with regard to the 2011 England tour. As it also administers the IPL, the board was unwilling to pull its players out of the tournament, careful as it was to make sure that the competition was seen as prestigious. Rather, the board chose to let the players, or their bodies, make the decision. But, by not forcing the players to skip the IPL, the BCCI gave its implicit approval. This meant that "The lure of money and the backing of the Indian Board... proved a greater incentive than commitment to their [the Indian players'] craft and the country," according to a post-mortem of the series by an Indian journalist, Pradeep Magazine. Their places in the Test team were not under threat owing to the fact that they would rather play in the IPL than report ready and fit for duty for an overseas tour. For Test cricket, the situation was serious. The England-India series was a prestigious one, encompassing four matches (which itself is an increasingly rare thing), with the world-number-one ranking at stake. It was supposed to pit the best team in the world against their biggest challengers, and represented the last chance for a generation of Indian batsman—Dravid, Tendulkar and VVS Laxman—to play in front of English crowds. The matches that followed were nothing short of a travesty. They made a mockery of the quality that gives Test cricket its integrity: the fact that it provides the sport's toughest examination. India, who had never previously lost a Test series under the captaincy of MS Dhoni, were in no shape to face England, and their tour schedule all but guaranteed it.

If a dramatisation of the tour were to be staged in the theatre, the director would have the choice between portraying it as a light farce or a tragedy. It began in disarray, with the late arrival of the Indians from the West Indies, which permitted them to play no more than one warm-up game, against Somerset, before the start of the Tests. A comparison with Ian Chappell's Australians is worth making. For one young batsman, Suresh Raina, it constituted a reasonable chance to stretch his legs—he scored a century and bowled 16 overs of off-breaks. However, for Laxman, captain and wicketkeeper Dhoni, leading spinner, Harbhajan Singh, and bowlers Praveen Kumar and Ishant Sharma, it was of no use at all, because they were not selected. This meant that these five men began the subsequent Test series without a single minute of competitive cricket in England. It is a wonder that India managed to tie England down as well as they did on that first day at Lord's, when England struggled to 127-2 off 49 tough and competitive overs.

By the end of the first day, however, England had already seen off India's best bowler, Zaheer Khan, whose hamstring withstood only 13 overs of bowling. A canny left-arm seamer with good variation, Zaheer relies more on swing than express pace to trouble batsman. He also has a tendency to carry a bit of extra weight on his midriff. This is not necessarily a problem, even for a fast bowler (ask, or perhaps don't ask, Australia's Merv Hughes), but it does indicate a need to manage his schedule and training carefully, particularly given his history of injuries. However, in the build-up to the England series, Zaheer endured a hectic period of four Tests and seven

ODIs against New Zealand and South Africa, nine appearances in the World Cup, followed by 15 games in the IPL, where his Royal Challengers were defeated in the final. He was then unable to travel to the Caribbean because of a knock to his right ankle. Nevertheless, he was judged to be sufficiently fit for the England tour, until his appearances at Somerset and at Lord's suggested that he was not in great shape. India's reluctance to rule him out of the tour following his breakdown in the First Test betrayed their reliance upon him. Initially, they said that he was out for the day, then for the match, then for the first two Tests and only admitted that he was to be sidelined for the whole series once he had failed completely in the practice game against Northants. Tellingly, it turned out that he needed not only rest for his hamstring, but also an operation on his troublesome ankle, suggesting that India had rushed him back before he was properly match fit.

Injuries to key players have a direct effect on the performance of their teammates. The loss of Zaheer in the First Test increased the workload of the two other fast bowlers, Sharma and the rookie, Kumar. In the first two Tests, the pair bowled a total of 223 overs. Anderson and Broad bowled the equivalent of two whole sessions fewer, with 174. In the Second Test at Nottingham, India's pace attack bowled beautifully to reduce England to 88-6 in the first innings, but were unable to exert sufficient pressure to finish the job, allowing England to recover to the relative safety of 221. Likewise, in the second innings, England were able to exploit Sharma and Kumar's wearying bodies to add 205 for the last four wickets, leaving India a notional 478 to win. England's bowlers were comparatively fresh, and had the energy to exploit the aversion of the Indian middle order to the short ball. Raina perished to the hook shot, Yuvraj Singh, who looked hopelessly uncomfortable in his first Test in a year, soon gloved one to silly point, while Dhoni made a dreadful error to be out lbw to his first ball. On an evening of urgent and aggressive bowling, India succumbed for just 158.

After two heavy defeats in quick succession, India needed some time to regroup, but their schedule did not permit such a luxury. Four days after the loss at Trent Bridge, they were playing Northants, and four days after that the Third Test began at Edgbaston. This is the problem of playing four Tests in a month: it is very difficult to devise new strategies or to lift the spirits. A former editor of *The Cricketer*, John Stern, was at Wantage Road and described how "In the field, India looked barely interested. On a breezy, cool day, fielders' hands were in pockets, the body language sheepish and bored. After tea, seven fours came from nine balls as India's out-cricket descended into schoolboy mode."

There was no visible improvement in morale at Edgbaston. As *The Guardian* reported pithily, "India's body language is desperate. If this were a film they would be played by William H Macy."

A tight schedule does not negate the differences between opponents, it magnifies them. For India, this meant that injuries did not have time to heal, and replacements did not have the chance to acclimatise, making it progressively easier for England to dominate. Before the start of the Second Test, India summoned, as cover for Zaheer, RP Singh, who had made an excellent impression as a young bowler when India toured England in 2007. Incredibly, neither the BCCI nor Singh himself had thought to apply for a visa, despite his status as one of the 30 Indian players contracted to play international cricket. With Singh temporarily unavailable, the selectors turned to Munaf Patel, another young gun who shone in 2007. He, at least, arrived for a day of play against Northants, but bowled risibly and was overlooked for the last two Tests. Singh eventually arrived and played in the Fourth Test, when the effects of a diet of nothing but T20 cricket were clear. *The Telegraph* reporter described how Singh "waddles to the wicket in the manner of a club seamer, his speed barely above military medium, the swing mainly onto the middle of the bat. He looked palpably unfit, as if he had spent most of his IPL money on *naan* bread." In India's innings defeat he bowled 34 innocuous overs and failed to take a wicket. Owing to an unbalanced schedule, a lack of competitive practice and some embarrassing administrative sloth, India ensured that their bowlers would take no more than 47 English wickets in four Tests.

Finally, there was Sachin. Not even he, the greatest batsman since Bradman, was able to thrive within the tight confines of this particular tour. After enduring a schedule comparably hectic to that of Zaheer, Tendulkar opted out of the trip to the West Indies, citing a desire to spend time with his family. Given that he had just played months of cricket in India, this seemed a strange decision. It also meant that the Lord's Test was the first that he had played for six months. As ever, he was at the centre of things in the build-up to the match, not least because he was on the threshold of becoming the first batsman to score 100 international centuries. For 90 minutes in the first innings he played as if he was struck by the enormity of what he was about to achieve, swishing uncharacteristically several times outside off-stump. He also hit two excellent boundaries off the back foot, but he was playing from memory rather than touch. When he had made 34, Broad had him caught at second slip. It was the first really good ball that Tendulkar had faced, full, fast and swinging away, and it betrayed the Little Master's rustiness. He was generally subdued for the rest of the series. There was another moment of excitement at The Oval, when he made 91, but it was a scratchy innings assisted by two drops and a missed stumping. His tour was a demonstration that even the best are hostage to the right preparation and management. Prior to arriving in England, the Indians had played too much of the wrong sort of cricket. They were both undercooked and exhausted.

Since the end of the England-India series, the sense of unease surrounding the scheduling of Test cricket has grown. In November 2011 Michael Clarke's Australians toured South Africa. Their itinerary comprised three T20s, three ODIs, a three-day tour match, and just two Tests. Before the series started, South African bowler, Dale Steyn, remarked caustically, "I go on holiday for longer than that series is going to last." It was a great one-liner, brimming with frustration and cynicism at the erosion of the game that he describes as the "ultimate". His teammate, Jacques Kallis, was in similarly gloomy mood: "If Test cricket is being compromised in any way, then I am dead against it. Everything comes from Test cricket, all the other formats of the game and the reputations that players gain, it all comes from playing—or aspiring to play—Test cricket. We know that, as players, we know how the game works." The reason that the series was chopped from three Tests to two was the scheduling of the Champions League T20 tournament, an anaemic attempt to replicate the success of UEFA's Champions League competition by pitting the champions of domestic T20 tournaments against each other. If you can remember the winning team of the 2011 competition, I'll be surprised.[2] The anger expressed by Kallis and Steyn was doubtless intensified by the confirmation that, in the eyes of the ICC, Test cricket had slid below not only ODIs and T20 internationals, but also domestic T20 competitions.

If the South African pair were keen to make a point, then they made it in the best possible way, by participating in two Tests of extraordinary drama. All that is thrilling about Test cricket was on show in Johannesburg and Cape Town. Given the cricket fan's love of an implausible victory, the events of the First Test are destined to become as familiar as those of Headingley in 1981 or Kolkata in 2001. Clarke asserted himself for the first time as captain with an exceptional 151, out of a slightly below-par Australian total of 284. But this was merely the beginning. On the second day, Shane Watson hustled South Africa out for 96, before South Africa's trio of Steyn, Morkel and debutant, Vernon Philander, ripped Australia apart. At 21 for 9, Australia were on the verge of rewriting a whole book of records for batting ineptitude, before a last-wicket partnership of 26 dragged them to the relatively banal awfulness of 47 all out. Amid a hysterical atmosphere, Graeme Smith and Hashim Amla found the composure to bat sensibly, hitting centuries in what turned out to be an emphatic 8-wicket win. The Second Test was a more traditional nerve-shredder. Australia were set 310 to win on the final day and managed to beat the enveloping darkness and a clatter of late wickets to win with two remaining, the decisive runs struck by their youngest-ever Test player, Pat Cummins, who was making his debut.

Such a brief summary does little to convey the joy of the series. It was tough cricket in places, as it ought to be between two streetwise teams. They appeared so evenly matched that some attritional sessions seemed likely. But the sudden tumble of wickets at Johannesburg turned the Test into a maelstrom that seemed likely to suck in every player, before Smith and Amla produced a masterpiece of

....

2   *I had to look it up, and apparently it was the Mumbai Indians.*

deception. Anyone who watched their partnership out of context would have been dumbstruck to learn that 22 wickets had fallen the previous day, such was their ability to bat unperturbed. There was also the enjoyable sensation of being offered a glimpse into the future. Cummins played with the maturity of a man a decade older than his 18 years to take six second-innings wickets and score his match-winning 13 not out, while Philander summoned prodigious swing to grab 14 wickets in the two matches.

But then it was over. No sooner had Cummins hit a four through midwicket to level the series at 1-1 than Australia were due back home to gear up for another two-Test series, this time against New Zealand.[3] Thrilling though the South Africa series undoubtedly was, no player, supporter or administrator would have been satisfied by its abrupt end, which was as unfathomable as the end of an English Premier League season after 19 matches or the ATP tour after the French Open. It is hard to conceive of another sport that does so much to deny its fans exciting matches. When I put a comment by the Australian bowler, Ryan Harris, who described the two-Test series as "pointless" to CA, a spokesman would say only that Australia is playing very few two-Test series until 2020. This isn't quite true: of the 33 Test series that Australia is scheduled to play between 2011 and 2020, seven, or almost one-quarter, are two Tests long. Having seen how Test match tours have changed in the past 40 years and explored the detrimental effects of the vogue for shorter, blink-and-you'll-miss-'em series, it is necessary to figure out how we got here.

Before the ICC took control of the international calendar, teams used to play each other whenever was convenient, which turned out to be more or less when the weather looked decent. The time and effort required to travel across the world meant that tours were not exactly *ad hoc* arrangements, but nor was there much fuss and bother about hurrying back in time to play the next opponents, as demonstrated by the Australians' baggy schedule in 1972. Since then, however, the advent of cricket as a spectator sport, watched not only by fans at the ground, but also by an exponentially larger

---

3   To add to the farce, five of the Australians who toured South Africa – Shane Watson, Ryan Harris, Shaun Marsh, Mitchell Johnson and Pat Cummins – were ruled out of the first game against New Zealand because there was insufficient time for their minor injuries to heal.

audience on television, has had a profound effect on the nature of the tour. So too has the ascension of Sri Lanka, Bangladesh and Zimbabwe to Test-playing status.

Minutes from a meeting of the chief executives of the ICC in 1997 reveal that there was sufficient concern about the reluctance of the established Test teams to travel to these emerging cricket nations and engage in "effective, interesting and commercially viable tour programmes" that it was felt that the development of the sport was being impeded. The subtext is that the broadcasting rights for the Ashes or for almost any series in India were huge, and getting bigger. However, as the earnings from travelling to Bangladesh to thrash Test cricket's newest minnows were miniscule, the larger teams were dragging their feet. The solution, proposed by New Zealand's Chris Doig, was the Future Tours Programme (FTP), a giant fixture-planner that ensures that each nation plays a home and an away Test series against every other nation over a five-year period. The national boards remained responsible for the length and frequency of the tours, but the ICC was ready to corral squabbling members into agreement if necessary. It also meant that broadcasters knew, long in advance, the cricket that was available to screen. The first iteration of the FTP covered the period from 2006 to 2012, and the second from 2011 to 2020.

Looking at the ICC's guidelines for the FTP, it becomes difficult to understand how Test cricket has got itself into such a mess. There are rules governing the number of back-to-back Tests that can be played, a minimum rest period between overseas tours and a limit on the number of ODIs a team can schedule in a year. It is impossible to imagine three more sensible rules, and there are others that are similarly well considered, giving the overall impression that the ICC thought hard about how to protect international cricketers from exhaustion. The guidelines were, however, drawn up before the globalisation of T20.

For such a short game, T20 has caused a disproportionate amount of trouble. The negotiations for the second FTP turned out to be a whole lot more difficult than the first, as national boards insisted on as much lucrative T20 as possible. This meant that the second FTP had to accommodate up to three T20 matches per tour, a biannual T20 World Cup, and, most superfluously, an annual T20 Champions

League. Although the IPL was not recognised in the calendar, the negotiators took heed of its existence. What has yielded, unsurprisingly, is the length of Test series.

Examples are easy to come by: South Africa were scheduled to play four series of at least four Tests in the six years of the first FTP. They will not play a single one in the first five years of the second. Odd matches have been lost everywhere: New Zealand's trip to Sri Lanka in 2012 was cut from three Tests to two, while the West Indies' home series against Australia in 2015 has been chopped from four to two. Four of the ten Test teams—the West Indies, Sri Lanka, Bangladesh and Zimbabwe—will not play a series longer than three Tests between now and 2020. There will also be just two series of five Tests, and not a single one that does not involve England. The sad irony of the FTP is that the ICC's biggest players were initially resistant to it, as they believed that it posed a threat to the prestige of the biggest series. They were right, but the threat was not the one that they imagined.

It is no exaggeration to suggest that the calendar outlined by the second FTP has trapped Test cricket in a downward spiral. It takes little imagination to see a decline, where shorter series lead to an erosion of basic skills; where batsmen forget how to occupy the crease without scoring at a run a ball; where bowlers forget how to put the ball in the same spot outside off stump; where touring teams do not have enough time to acclimatise to make matches competitive; where a series of one-sided matches leads to crowds staying away; where more ODIs and T20s have to be scheduled to make up for the decline in Test match revenue; where the amount of time for Test cricket is squeezed further; where the next generations of fans grow up having never seen cricket played in whites. It is not inconceivable—indeed some would say it was more than likely—that the fifth or sixth FTP will schedule only a few one-off Test matches. These would be sepia-tinged affairs, played as a concession to the sport's few remaining traditionalists, a mild diversion before cricketers and fans get back to the real business of T20.

There is no doubt that the first step in the decline is already happening. The helter-skelter cricket played in Tests between England and India and Australia and South Africa makes a lot more sense when seen in the context of players grappling with the demands of a sport that is no longer familiar to them. As long ago as the 2009 Ashes Gideon Haigh spotted

"two teams stretched in ways quite unfamiliar to them, like teenagers being expected to graduate from SMS to iambic pentameters—and it showed. The wins were conquests. The losses were capitulations. The batting collapses were ruinous and utter. The bowling collapses—see [Mitchell] Johnson at Lord's, [Monty] Panesar at Cardiff—were complete. Have teams played more contrasting consecutive Tests than Headingley and the Oval? [Australia won by an innings in Leeds; England by 197 runs in London.] Have teams struggled as much with putting consecutive deliveries in the same place?"

It is possible that this series was just an oddity, where the all-consuming nature of the Ashes overwhelmed the players, but the subsequent low-grade (if occasionally thrilling) Test cricket that has been seen since suggests that it was the beginning of a now-established trend.

Before accepting that the current scheduling of cricket, across all its formats, will consign Test cricket to the dustbin, it is worth acknowledging some pockets of resistance. The first signs of a backlash came in the aftermath of the 2006-07 Ashes, which saw England, under the command of stand-in captain, Andrew Flintoff, humiliated by Australia. Such was the desperation of the tour that the England and Wales Cricket Board (ECB) commissioned a review of how the team was managed before the Fifth Test had even begun.

The subsequent report, led by a former head of golf's European Tour, Ken Schofield, described how England's preparations were "compromised by the ICC's scheduling of the Champions Trophy [an international ODI tournament] so close to the same organisation's World Cup that the traditional timing of and preparation for the five Test matches was advanced and condensed into the shortest period of time in the history of the contest". England played three matches in Australia before the First Test in Brisbane. The first was the traditional one-day warm-up in Canberra against a Prime Minister's XI, a fixture comparable with the Australians' game with the Duke of Norfolk's XI in terms of lack of intensity. The second was a 14-a-side, three-day stroll against New South Wales, and the third a three-day match against South Australia, during which England batted once in a tame draw. None of the games was given first-class status. This was particularly shoddy given that none of England's top seven—Strauss, Cook, Ian Bell, Paul Collingwood, Pietersen, Flintoff and Geraint Jones—had ever played a Test match in Australia. It was a team "not so much undercooked as blood-raw", according to former captain, Michael Atherton.

Among the Schofield Report's many and wide-ranging recommendations was that England should play three four-day first-class matches ahead of the 2010/11 Ashes in Australia. In the event, this was one of the Report's few recommendations that was not implemented precisely—England played two three-day matches and one four-day game—but more rigorous preparation contributed to a disciplined and professional performance unrecognisable from that of four years earlier. As important as the scheduling of these matches was the attitude of the England team towards them. They are now highly competitive encounters, not simply a chance to stretch the legs and soak up some winter sun. There was a touch of irony in the fact that England's 3-1 win in the 2010/11 Ashes prompted CA to do some soul-searching of its own, commissioning the Argus Review to investigate the declining fortunes of its Test team. Much like the Schofield Report, the Argus Review recommended bold changes to the selection and management structures—which were quickly adopted by CA—but was more circumspect on the scheduling and volume of matches. The dilemma faced by the governing body was outlined succinctly:

"The panel acknowledges the strategic importance of T20 for attracting new fans to cricket and the scheduling challenges presented by the resulting expansion of the Big Bash League [BBL, the domestic T20 competition] and the presence of Champions League T20 in September/October. At the same time, the panel notes international cricket, and Test cricket in particular, remains the highest priority. CA will therefore need to be creative about its domestic scheduling, with the balance of BBL fixtures—which attract new fans—and first-class fixtures—which develop players for international cricket—to be carefully managed."

The review went so far as to offer a suggestion of how CA could be "creative" in its scheduling. It proposed that the expanded BBL be held a month earlier, in December and January, to cash in on higher attendances over the Christmas holiday period. CA readily agreed, and the decision was seemingly justified by impressive television audiences, a series of sell-out crowds in the smaller grounds, and an attendance of almost 50,000 in the Melbourne Cricket Ground (MCG) for the match between the two Melbourne teams. There was a catch, however, and it was a big one.

An unavoidable consequence of the Argus Report's recommendation was that the BBL clashed with the summer Test series, and indeed the Boxing Day Test—the most famous event in the Australian cricket calendar. It was akin to scheduling Wimbledon at the same time as the French Open, or the Ryder Cup at the same time as the USPGA. Instead of uniting a growing cricket audience between two flagship events, CA elected to force Australian fans to choose between them. The matches suffered too: the BBL was deprived of the Australian Test captain, Clarke, who decided that a four-Test series was enough to keep him occupied, while other Test players, such as Michael Hussey and Shaun Marsh, played BBL matches as and when they could. Unsurprisingly, Clarke chose to keep his thoughts on his team's involvement in the BBL to himself, but it strained credulity that, at a time when Australian Test cricket was struggling, he could not count on his players' undivided attention.

Despite some occasionally dubious recommendations, such reviews are worthwhile if they force governing bodies into making commitments to which they would not otherwise agree. Pressure can then be applied if these promises do not materialise. The idea of the "icon series" is one such commitment. It was discussed widely by the ECB, BCCI, CA and Cricket South Africa (CSA), before being quietly hidden away in a cupboard when the negotiations proved tricky. It is well worth dragging it out and dusting it down.

In early 2009 the ECB took the laudable step of announcing that it wished to lengthen Test series between England and India from three to five matches. Relations between the ECB and BCCI were particularly strong at that point, as England had agreed to play two rescheduled Test matches in India that were moved following the Mumbai bombings. The BCCI accepted—despite India having not played a five-Test series since 2002—and this led to a fourth Test being added to India's 2011 tour and a fifth Test to their visits in 2014 and 2018. In addition, England tours to India in 2012 and 2016 were lengthened to four Tests. For a brief moment it seemed as if the idea of the icon series was about to become fashionable. In the summer of 2008 the president of the CSA, Norman Arendse, described the granting of icon status to Test matches between England and South Africa as "a wonderful recognition of the standard of South African cricket". But such resolve wilted when it came to the scheduling of the second FTP, and so England played just three Tests against South Africa in 2012, alongside a seven-match ODI series against Australia. When asked what the one-day matches were doing, sitting so incongruously in the schedule, an ECB spokesman responded:

"We are keen to schedule in an ODI series next summer against Australia for cricketing reasons, rather than an additional Test match. This will be a reciprocal ODI series, which means we can then play an ODI series in Australia immediately prior to the next Cricket World Cup in Australia and NZ in 2015, assisting with our preparation and acclimatisation for the tournament. The England team management had also requested, after our poor performance in the Cricket World Cup in 2007, that we needed to play more ODI cricket to compete effectively with other leading nations who play more of this type of cricket."

In other words, it is another example of Tests being chopped to make room for shorter forms of the game. Incidentally, the ECB seems to have forgotten entirely that, in the press release it issued in 2008, it said that England-South Africa series were to be five, not four matches in length. The fifth match appears to have been lost in the ether. The idea of giving extra protection to a limited number of Test series is a good one. It is not without fault: the most high-profile series are the ones that are most likely to survive, as they generate the greatest amount of revenue. Those that are under the greatest threat are those that are three or four Tests long and face cutting to two or three. The icon idea shows that country boards are not totally unaware of the threats facing Tests, but also that their desire to protect them is limited.

A three-Test series is "the minimum you need to test the skills and depth of two teams", according to the South African former opening batsman, Gary Kirsten. Kirsten is one of many current or recently retired players who have felt moved to comment on the danger posed to Test cricket by the current international schedule. Others have included Strauss, Smith and Gilchrist. None, however, has used a platform so high-profile as that adopted by Dravid, when he outlined the difficulties facing Test cricket at the 2011 Bradman Lecture in Canberra. He acknowledged the importance of ODIs and T20 in maintaining revenue, but warned that cricket "must scale down this mad merry-go-round that teams and players find themselves in: heading off for two-Test tours and seven-match ODI series, with a few T20s thrown in. Test cricket deserves to be protected; it is what the world's best know they will be judged by". He also addressed the prophecy made earlier in this chapter of poor-quality games driving fans away: "We may not fill 65,000-capacity stadiums for Test matches, but we must actively fight to get as many as we can in, to create a Test match environment that the players and the fans feed off. Anything but the sight of Tests played on empty grounds." Dravid is also a member of the MCC's World Cricket Committee, a group of 19 cricket luminaries that meets biannually to chew the fat on the state of the game. It was likely to have been no coincidence that committee expressed its "disappointment" at the shift towards shorter Test series, after a recent meeting in Cape Town.

This, then, is the sum of the resistance to the current downward spiral of Test cricket: a couple of independent reviews, a few promises between cricket boards and the resolve of some recent Test players. It is both meagre and a starting point for the future. Pressure on the scheduling of Test matches is only going to intensify in the coming years. The shift towards lucrative short matches is continuing apace. In early 2012 Sri Lanka Cricket, still struggling with the cost of refurbishing the ground in Colombo that was used in the 2011 World Cup, successfully petitioned the BCCI to play three ODIs on its forthcoming tour to Sri Lanka, rather than the three Tests previously agreed, in order to maximise revenue. For as long as moves like this are made, advocates of Test cricket will need to become more effective cheerleaders for the sport.

The yardstick for their success is likely to be the fate of the mooted World Test Championship. Like most ideas in Test cricket, it is not new—it was first proposed in *Wisden Cricket Monthly* back in the 1990s. The theory is that Test cricket struggles, both in comparison with ODIs and T20, and with other sports, because it lacks a show-piece event that draws in casual viewers in the manner of the football and rugby world cups. The fact that these competitions are global means that winners' medals are more coveted among players than any other, while for administrators there are broadcasting rights to be sold across the world. Test cricket has no equivalent competition. The series between England and India was a *de facto* world cup final—the accolade for the best team in the world was at stake—but the result was of little consequence in Sri Lanka or the West Indies.

The World Test Championship would go some way to fixing this problem by inviting the four highest-ranked teams to play three one-off Test matches—two semi-finals and a final—every four years. This is a very exciting idea. There is the potential for some dramatic and high-quality cricket. Imagine a scene at Lord's where Australia set England a target of 300 to win in the fourth innings on a pitch that has begun to turn; imagine the nervous energy in the crowd as the home side lose a couple of early wickets; the sun beginning to set behind the pavilion as 50 are needed from the last three wickets. The reality might be more humdrum, but the potential for a thrilling game would still draw in big crowds and high viewing figures. The championship would also give greater relevance to other series played in the months before, as teams attempted to secure the ranking points needed to qualify. And, perhaps most significantly of all, it would force a re-evaluation of the FTP, which would have to be shifted to a four-year cycle. This opportunity would allow Test cricket to push back against the tide of ODIs and T20 and redress years of imbalance.

Yet even some self-proclaimed advocates of Test cricket are not convinced. In 2010 a former editor of *Wisden*, Scyld Berry, suggested that the championship "would violate one of cricket's most funda-mental values. It would be unfair". He continues: "Your country has sweated for four years to reach No1 in the Test rankings. In the semi-final—a one-off Test match—you face No 4. You bat first on one of those cloudy mornings... and the ball hoops around, before the sun comes out when your opponents take to the crease. Four years' work down the pan in a session: how fair is that?"

This view is flawed, as competitive sport is not, by its very nature, inherently fair. Rugby games are affected by the wind, football matches by the state of the pitch, Formula 1 races by the rain—and these factors tend not to affect each player or team equally. Cricket can feel particularly unfair, given the heavy influence of the weather on playing conditions. However, in each of these sports, coping with the weather or the hostility of the crowd is one of the skills required. If total fairness were essential, matches ought to take place in a vacuum. This is nonsense. There is a strong chance that a World Test Championship would be won by a team that was not top of the rankings. But that does not deter the best teams in football or rugby from participating in tournaments, because it is more rewarding to play in a tough competition and risk defeat than to come out on top on a Monday morning when an unknown statistician runs an algorithm. A more realistic concern is that it feels incongruous to promote Test cricket—a game that works best when played over a whole summer—through three one-off matches. But a short, effectively marketed championship could rekindle interest in the five-day game by providing a hook from which to hang the rest of the calendar. The benefits could lessen Test cricket's dependence on ODIs and T20. The championship is not an ideal solution, but it has come at a time when pragmatism is required.

Or, it may not come at all. In November 2011 the then ICC chief executive, Haroon Lorgat, announced that the championship had been postponed from 2013 to 2017, a decision that was "a reality of the commitments that we've got already through to 2015". These commitments do not relate to finding a gap in a tight schedule, but to the broadcasting-rights deal agreed with ESPN Star Sports, who bought the global rights to the ICC's event until 2015. The ICC proposed to ESPN Star Sports that the World Test Championship should replace the unloved ODI Champions Trophy, the next instalment of which took place England in 2013. (As a measure of its relevance, I again challenge you to name the winners of the 2009 tournament.[4]) The broadcaster is believed to have told the ICC that it would pay a smaller fee for the championship than for the Champions Trophy because of concerns about its global appeal, and the ICC's members were unwilling to sanction the consequent fall in revenue.

This was a distressing development, not least because it is so easy to imagine the situation repeating itself in four years' time. As Test cricket becomes less commercially viable, ESPN or its successor would find the same deal less palatable. The onus will once

---

4   *The winners were Australia, who beat New Zealand by six wickets in Centurion.*

again fall on the ICC and its members, and by then any impetus to keep Test cricket healthy may have been lost for good. This, then, is the unhappy present. Pockets of resistance, small but committed, remain in the fight to return Test cricket to its former glory. These advocates have wised up, and their demands are reasonable. There is now widespread acknowledgment that long series of matches between every Test nation are neither possible nor desirable. But nor are the two-Test time-wasting tours that litter the FTP, or the inadequate preparations that ruin the few traditional tours that remain. At the end of the stunted series between Australia and South Africa, a wag suggested to Clarke that the Australian flights home had been cancelled, and a third Test had been arranged. Without missing a beat, he replied, "When can we start?"

Chapter Two
The Short Game

> *"I just can't tell how good Chris Gayle is.*
> *And I'm disappointed about that."*
>
> *Gideon Haigh*
>
> . . . .

Interviewing modern sportsmen and women can be a thankless task. With agents and PR and media managers ubiquitous, teasing out an interesting sound bite requires patience, persistence and often a little cheek. Cricketers, while typically more eloquent than most professional sportspeople, are no different. A writer would have to get up very early to catch the England captain, Alastair Cook, going off-message. All credit then, to *The Observer*'s Anna Kessel, who in May 2009 was granted an interview with the then Test captain of the West Indies, Chris Gayle. Laid-back to the point of semi-consciousness, Gayle only really looks animated when he sees a fast bowler drop the ball short. Then, he raises his unusually high back-lift even higher, shuffles to his right to give himself room and hurls his bat through a violent arc. In such circumstances, the ball tends to land in the top tier of the stand, on the stadium roof, or, as was the case during one unfortunate incident in 2012, on the nose of a young female fan.

When Kessel met Gayle in his hotel in London, he was grumpy, and with good reason. No sooner had he landed in England than he found himself roundly criticised in the press. His commitments to the Kolkata Knight Riders in the Twenty20 (T20) Indian Premier League (IPL) meant that he arrived in the country less than 48 hours before the start of the Test series, which the English press decried as evidence of a lack of commitment. His conduct was questioned by his opposite number, Andrew Strauss. Gayle's cause was not helped by the fact that his team then slumped to a 10-wicket defeat in less than three days in the First Test, and he made just 28 runs in two innings. By Kessel's account, during their hour-long conversation, only a mug of hot chocolate brought a smile to his face. Yet, from his gloomy introspection, she managed to draw an admission that he was keen to shed the captaincy, the demands of which were never compatible with the instinctive way in which he plays cricket, and also a much bigger revelation, that he "wouldn't be so sad" if Test cricket died.

This admission ruffled far more feathers than his lack of preparation for the Test series. Two former captains of Australia, Ian Chappell and Mark Taylor, suggested he should resign. A third, Kim Hughes, described him and his team as an "embarrassment". He also received little sympathy from senior figures in the West Indies and England. To some, however, Gayle had good reason to feel dissatisfied. An interminable series of contractual disputes between the dysfunctional West Indies Cricket Board (WICB) and the West Indies Players' Association has stymied the recovery retarded the team in the past decade, with players striking and the WICB issuing criticism in the media. A successful captain nowadays needs needed to be as competent a diplomat as a cricketer. The series against England also felt like an imposition on the tourists. Gayle and his team were packed off across the Atlantic in chilly May because the Sri Lankans had refused to tour, citing the proximity of the IPL, only for the compliant West Indians to find their hosts questioning the captain's commitment once they got there. It was not an environment conducive to tough, competitive Test cricket. But it was not the weariness of leading a team in decline on an unwanted tour that was behind Gayle's downbeat attitude towards five-day cricket. Instead, his head had been turned by what he had seen in the IPL in South Africa. His mind had become fixed on T20.

In June 2013 T20 celebrated its tenth birthday. In those ten years it has redefined the sport entirely. No corner of the game has been left untouched, from its global administration to the size of its bats; from the teams its spectators cheer to the amount of money its players earn. T20 has lit a fire under cricket's sluggish governing body, the International Cricket Council (ICC), transferred huge power to its players and has shifted cricket's centre of power from London to Mumbai.

Yet nothing has evolved faster than the T20 form of the game itself. The mundanity of its origins gave little indication of the behemoth that it was to become. In 2003 the England and Wales Cricket Board

(ECB) needed a new game to replace the ailing Benson & Hedges Cup, which, after a slow drift into obscurity, was finally sunk by a government ban on tobacco sponsorship at sporting events. The counties chose to fill the gaps in their schedules (and the holes in their balance sheets) with what was literally a marketing man's dream. An unlikely man to change the future of a global sport, an ECB executive, Stuart Robertson, sold them on the virtues of a shorter game, pitched at the after-work crowd. That the inaugural T20 Cup was approved owed less to any great faith that it would succeed than the counties' desperation to arrest what they feared was a terminal decline in attendances.

It is a measure of how T20 has developed that reports of its opening weekend sound like telegrams from a bygone age; Hampshire played Sussex in the first game and fielded a pace attack of Ed Giddins, Alan Mullally and Wasim Akram; Gloucestershire got into the spirit by threatening to ban any members who wore a tie; Worcestershire decided that what the game really needed was a hot tub jacuzzi on the boundary; while Surrey captain, Adam Hollioake, chose to bowl first on winning the toss "because I haven't a clue what is going to happen". If this all sounds rather innocent and quaint, it is because it was. The first season of T20 in England showed the new game to be a gimmick, albeit a popular one. The average crowd at the 45 matches played that season was 5,300, compared with a daily gate of 880 in the County Championship the previous year, according to research by William Buckland. County grounds dusted down "sold-out" signs that had not been used for decades.

Since then, T20 has progressed from the hazy, village-fete atmosphere of the English county summer to become the embodiment of cricket's brash modernisation, the game on fast-forward and in a tight embrace with its commercial partners. It has also become the cuckoo in the nest of the ICC's international schedule. New tournaments and cups have been hatched that compete for fans' attention and broadcasters' revenue with Tests and one-day internationals (ODIs). This transformation needed an architect, and preferably someone yet to have been lulled by the soporific rhythms of cricket administration. That man, of course, was Lalit Modi. After a privileged upbringing and an expensive education in India and the US (where his career at Duke University was cut short by a criminal conviction for attempting to traffic cocaine), he launched himself into the business world, equipped with enough family money to take risks, but not so much as to diminish his need to prove his worth. No profile of Modi has been written without reference to his prodigious work rate, and enough accounts exist of him going several days without sleep and phoning up associates in the dead of night to suggest that there must be some truth in the portrayal. However, as important to his success in transforming T20 was his status as a cricket outsider. He dabbled in cricket as a young man, but in an interview with *Tehelka* in 2006 admitted that he was not a talented player. There was also little in his early business ventures that indicated any particular interest in cricket. He worked for Philip Morris and Estée Lauder before moving on to selling television rights. This failure to immerse himself in cricket eventually proved advantageous. The sport's slavish dedication to tradition, fascination with its forebears and stubborn resistance to change is a powerful drug that holds most cricket men and women contentedly under sedation. But Modi did not grow up so intoxicated, and therefore was untroubled by rewriting cricket culture—particularly when he saw that there was money to be made.

His great innovation was to divorce cricket from its fusty admin-istration and obsession with the past and marry it instead to the ethos of the free market. It was an idea that pre-dated the invention of T20. As long ago as 1995 Modi tried to interest Indian cricket's administrative body, the Board of Control for Cricket in India (BCCI), in the idea of an inter-city league, but was given short shrift. He recognised that first-class cricket, as it continues to be played all over the world, is governed by what economists would recognise as non-tariff barriers, the sort of restrictions that India specialised in under the stultifying Licence Raj. There is no free movement of labour: the majority of players sign up for their local county or team. There are strict limits on the number of overseas imports in order to protect domestic interests. Only once local players are good enough are they permitted to travel abroad to represent their country. When he established the IPL, Modi dispensed with all of this. Franchises were created out of thin air and sold to the highest bidders. Players were invited from all over the world to appear in the IPL auction catalogue, but were instructed to come as individuals; the IPL refuses to recognise player representatives, agents, lawyers or associations. Once they were committed, players were sold according to what the market said they were worth. Those that performed well saw their price rise in subsequent years; those that disappointed saw their stock plummet. And, as has been seen the world over, from Eastern Europe to Latin America to South-East Asia, when the barriers to trade come down, the money rushes in.

And so it did, in unprecedented amounts. In the last pre-IPL television-rights deal, the BCCI sold global media rights to the Indian Test and one-day teams for four years to Nimbus for US$621m. In comparison, Modi sold the ten-year global rights for the IPL—before a ball had been bowled or a team had been created—to a consortium of Sony and Singapore's World Sports Group for over US$1bn (after a legal dispute, this figure rose above US$1.5bn). Around three-quarters of this sum were to be paid to the owners of the franchises; around one-fifth would be ploughed back into the IPL and around one-twelfth would form the prize money. The ICC, who watched this unfold in its back garden, received nothing.

Less than a week later, Modi put his franchises up for sale, each with a base price of US$50m. Aside from a cut of the television rights, the franchises had no assets. They existed only as figments of their owner's imagination. There were no players, no staff, no ground and no sponsors. If he was worried, he had no need to be. Bollywood and business were receptive. The Jaipur team, at US$67m, ended up as the cheapest franchise, while Indian's richest man, Mukesh Ambani, CEO of Reliance Industries, spent US$111.9m on the rights to a team in Mumbai. The sale raised US$723.6m, against a base price of US$400m. Further cash soon rolled in from sponsors: naming rights to a local real-estate developer for US$50m and sponsorship deals with global telecoms and banks for another US$150m. By opening up cricket to all who could afford a piece of it, the IPL has become the richest game in town.

When asked by *Tehelka* for his philosophy, Modi replied: "I believe in free markets deciding everything. Let people decide. In certain cases you might lose, in certain cases you might win". Unsurprisingly, the commitment of Modi and the BCCI to this philosophy was undermined as soon as it was tested. Subsequent events showed that the BCCI preferred the idea of creating a free market for its products, rather than for its products to compete in a free market. Since the IPL was established, Modi, with the confidence of a huge emerging political and economic power coursing through his veins, abandoned almost all free-market principles. In the words of Gideon Haigh, the IPL is a "perfectly brutal monopolist". One suspects this was always Modi's intention. It can hardly have been any other way, as, in spite of the creation of T20 tournaments in Australia, Sri Lanka and Bangladesh, there is only room in the international schedule for one event of the size of the IPL, which now encompasses more than 70 matches over seven weeks. Players who had competed in a pre-cursor to the IPL, the Indian Cricket League (ICL), were banned by the BCCI from playing in the IPL, while it declared that its stadiums and facilities were also off-limits to the ICL's organisers. Michael Atherton reported on one of the more ludicrous examples of the IPL erecting barriers around its product: "In New Zealand... Sachin Tendulkar was withdrawn from a charity match because of the contaminating presence of an ICL player in the same fixture".

The full extent of Lalit Modi's betrayal of his free-market philosophy was only revealed once his downfall had begun. Immediately after the end of the third instalment of the IPL in April 2010 the BCCI voted to suspend him from his dual role as the league's chairman and commissioner, following an exposé by *The Times of India*. The paper claimed access to a report compiled by the Indian income-tax department, which alleged that Modi held silent stakes in three IPL teams and had received under-the-table payments from several of the league's rights-holders. There were also uncomfortably close links between IPL franchises and Modi's friends and family. Rather than answer the charges of criminal conspiracy, cheating and falsification of accounts that were laid against him by police in Chennai, Modi chose to leave India for London; his dethronement as the king of Indian cricket was complete. Like many a monarch toppled by a coup, he is unhappy in exile, his influence on the sport reduced to a Twitter account from which he criticises the BCCI. But, even without a conviction or a proper hearing of the charges against him, the idea that the sale of the IPL franchises was conducted in accordance with free-market principles has been exposed as a hopeless illusion.

Another economic concept familiar to the BCCI is the idea of a national champion, a company or a conglomerate that is expected both to turn a profit and to advance the cause of its home country. Part of the strength and the resilience of the IPL in its first decade has come from the fact that it is not only a successful private enterprise, but that it has also come to represent India's arrival as a global economic power. Modi made this association in the aftermath of the first IPL: "It is a global representation of India and what the modern-day India stands for and its successes." And he is right. It took the vision and energy of a man from an emerging economy to take an experimental idea from England and explode it into something of formidable size and influence. The IPL as we know it could not and did not exist in any other country but India. The fanaticism of the country's cricket audience made bidding for the broadcasting rights a fairly safe bet. The growing wealth of these supporters made selling advertising space to global firms eager for a larger share of the Indian market a cinch. The size of the project fascinated the country's tycoons and entertainers. The promise of riches in a sport that has rarely paid well brought in many of the world's best players. This combination of demographics, entrepreneurship and enthusiasm is uniquely Indian.

But the embracing of the IPL as part of India's national character has created a number of serious problems for T20 and the wider cricket world. The IPL has been too successful for the good of anyone but itself and the BCCI. The commercial strength of the IPL has given the BCCI control over the international schedule. No broadcaster wants to bid for a Test series that competes against the IPL. No national cricket board wants to force its players to decide between an IPL contract and Test cricket, partly because they know which their players will choose. As Kevin Pietersen explained: "Some part of international cricket may have to give because the IPL is not going away. No one in their right mind would turn down the contracts I have been offered." Furthermore, the disparity between the revenue received by the BCCI and its contemporaries, particularly in Pakistan, Sri Lanka and the West Indies, is ruining any pretence that cricket has to being a level playing field. However, for the BCCI to cede control of the IPL to the ICC, where revenue stands a greater chance of being distributed equally and where the calendar could be planned centrally, is unthinkable. The IPL isn't just a premier league; it's the *Indian* Premier League. Until the national-champion model is discredited, the IPL will promote India primarily and cricket a very distant second.

As it enters its second decade, T20 is showing little signs of burn-out. It has shrugged off the initial snobbery from the media about the quality of the cricket (no less a figure than Michael Holding said: "Youngsters need to learn good techniques—they cannot do that by watching rubbish. There is nothing good about T20 cricket."), the temporary relocation of the IPL to South Africa in 2009 following the terrorist attacks on Mumbai, the coup against Modi, the grubby alliance with Allen Stanford, the disgraced US businessman now in jail for fraud, and the dilution of the game that has occurred through copycat tournaments springing up in Australia, Sri Lanka and Bangladesh. So far, it has also coped with its biggest challenge, of simply keeping the momentum going. T20, which feels most authentic when it is played in India, encapsulates that country's Gatsby age, a time of unprecedented wealth and self-congratulation. But even outside of the IPL, T20 demands "an atmosphere of constant celebration", according to Gideon Haigh, and this will be difficult to sustain. So, too, will be the novelty. T20 is built on cricket that is faster, bigger, louder. But novelty does not necessarily breed longevity. In Sydney, the Australian journalist, Malcolm Knox, illustrated this to me in such a way that it is worth quoting at length:

"In 2011 I took my son, a fairly typical nine-year-old boy with a short attention span, to a day of the Australia versus India Test match in Sydney and to a T20 international between the same teams. His reaction was the opposite to what you would expect. In the Test match he was intent for a while, drifted out for a while, drifted back in, got himself something to eat, came back, read a bit. As it happened, the rhythm of the day built up towards greater excitement and in the last session he was riveted. He said it was the best day of his life. At the T20, he and his mate were quite fixed on the game for the first 45 minutes, but, by the time the Indian innings was halfway through, they were bored and restless and wanted to leave. The volume had started so high and then had nowhere to go. Your expectation is set so high that not only are you expecting to see a six every over, but, if you do see a six every over, they just become humdrum and lose their effect."

The first ten years of T20 have brought a new set of conflicts to cricket. The calendar has come under pressure like never before; the rise of the franchise has imported from other sports the difficult issue

of club-versus-country; players and administrators have clashed more
vociferously and regularly; pubs, bars and cricket clubs have hosted
a decade-long argument between fans about the value of the shortest
form of the game. T20 has also brought about tremendous technical innovation: the quality of fielding across every form of cricket
has improved, almost beyond recognition; spin bowling has been
reborn as a method of taking wickets; and batsmen now use all 360
degrees of the pitch to score runs. But the story of how T20—with
the IPL at its core—has muscled in on international cricket is also
the story of how the Test match has changed in the past decade. It
is now not only possible to think of Test cricket as at a new stage
in its history, it is inconceivable to think of it in any other way. It is
now operating in the age of the short game.

If T20 has had a single, overwhelming effect on Test cricket in the
past decade, it has been the power that it has passed on to the players.
If the Packer crisis bruised national cricket boards in the 1970s, then
T20 has drawn blood. Once the dust settled on World Series Cricket,
players found themselves playing the same game, against the same
opponents, on the same grounds, only with more money in their
pockets. The effect of T20 has been more profound. A dichotomy
has been created between the old guard, comprising the ICC and
the national boards that trot out the oft-repeated line about the
primacy of Test cricket, and the thrusting new franchises that pay
huge wages for cricketers' short-term loyalty. Caught in the middle
are the players. Some have declined to explore their options, perhaps
because of a lack of interest in T20, the knowledge that their style
is not suited to the shortest form, an unwillingness to rock the boat
with their governing body, or a combination of all three. But those
that have embraced T20 franchises (as opposed to international T20
matches, which are built into the ICC's global schedule) have found
their national boards unable to push back.

The former New Zealand captain, Daniel Vettori, who is nobody's
idea of a rebel, was among a group of six Test players who spent two

weeks "agonising" in 2009, when New Zealand Cricket (NZC) asked its players to sign a national contract to play in a Test series against Australia that overlapped with the IPL. The group eventually decided to forgo the IPL, but Vettori felt the need to speak out, telling the press: "Our priority was to play for New Zealand, but we realise that, if these situations continue to come up, it will be difficult for players to continue to turn down the money... If Bangladesh were here it might have been an easier decision for players." As warnings go, it was pretty thinly veiled. A new era of player power had arrived, and it would be them that decided which Test matches they played in. The following year, NZC conceded and an eight-year agreement was signed with the national players' association that pledged a Test-free five-week window in the country's international schedule.[1]

Alone among national boards, the ECB has attempted to take a tougher line on the IPL. The central contracts negotiated by the ECB and the players' association permit English Test players three weeks of leave to participate in the IPL, which, given that the competition runs for seven weeks, means that English players are less attractive at auction, as they are not available for the business end of the tournament. It also means that players return from India before the end of the competition to play a single county match, a *de facto* warm-up, before the first Test of the summer. Under the ECB's contract with Sky, the ECB must host seven Test matches during the English summer, which limits the flexibility of the governing body. It has managed to hold relatively firm against the IPL because of the high regard in which Test matches are held in England, and the value of its deal with Sky, which helps it to narrow the disparity between earnings from Tests and earnings from the IPL. Nevertheless, even in the ECB's advantageous position, there is tension just below the surface. In August 2012 a brouhaha erupted over Kevin Pietersen's future in cricket. Although not confirmed in public, Pietersen wished to play the full IPL in 2013—earning his full £1.3m contract in the process—but the ECB refused to blink. After six days of thinking, he backed down and reconfirmed his commitment to England. But it

....

1   *This might sound like NZC doing all it can to protect Test cricket. But it did not negotiate with its future opponents to ensure that Tests could be moved. As a result, Vettori & Co again faced a choice between playing in the IPL in 2013 and playing a Test series in England.*

would be naive not to expect more conflicts in the future; Pietersen was simply the first in the England dressing room to speak out.

Other national cricket boards have been simply powerless. What incentives could the WICB offer to Chris Gayle to prevent him from becoming the first high-profile international freelance cricketer? Putting the board's own dysfunction aside, Gayle was faced with a choice between leading a struggling team around the world for three or four more years and losing more matches than he would win, or taking control of his future and maximising his earnings. His nomadic career now looks more akin to that of a journeyman footballer than an elite cricketer. In the past eight years he has turned out for the West Indies Test, one-day and T20 national teams; Jamaica, in the West Indies first-class domestic league; Worcestershire, in the County Championship; the Kolkata Knight Riders in the IPL, followed by a transfer to Royal Challengers Bangalore; the Matabeleland Tuskers in Zimbabwe's Logan Cup; the Warriors and then Sydney Thunder in Australia's T20 Big Bash League; and, most recently, Barisal Burners in the Bangladesh Premier League. He would have added another, had injury not prevented him from playing for Uva Next in the inaugural Sri Lanka Premier League.

Of course, Gayle has the added motivation of being one of T20's hottest tickets. The IPL sometimes gives the impression that its contracts are thrown around like confetti, but this isn't entirely fair. At the 2012 auction, players of the calibre of Graeme Swann, Ian Bell, VVS Laxman, Mark Boucher and Ajantha Mendis failed to find a team. Gayle himself missed out on an initial contract in 2011, although the WICB's subsequent failure to pick him for a series against Pakistan meant that he was soon back in India, playing for the Royal Challengers. It was in this, the fourth iteration of the IPL, that Gayle began to build a reputation as T20's master batsman, as opposed to simply its biggest biffer. His statistics for the 2011 and 2012 IPLs are otherworldly. In 26 innings he scored 1,341 runs at an average of 64 and at a strike rate of almost 172. No other batsman made 1,000 runs. Of the 788 balls he faced, 102 went for four and 103 went for six. He hit 44 sixes in 2011, which was more than any batsman hit in both years combined. And then he followed that up with 56 in 2012.

In an article on his blog, The Old Batsman argues that Gayle's recent unparalleled success in T20 was the result of more than just fortunate slogging: "Because the T20 game is shortened and heightened, his refinements are harder to spot, but they are there. His 128 not out from 62 [balls] against Delhi illustrated perfectly his current thinking. He didn't score from his first eight deliveries, and by the end of the first powerplay had 10 from 17. In his 'berserk' 57 from 31 against Pune, he had four from his first eight deliveries and 17 from his first 16." Gayle approaches his innings in T20 as any Test batsman plans his innings in a five-day game. He gives himself a sighting of the bowling, the pitch and the ground to reduce the risk of getting out through a misjudgement. He feels he can afford to do this, when most other batsmen are too concerned about maintaining the run rate, because of his extraordinary ability to go on and hit boundaries consistently. In the short history of T20, these two attributes, one mental and one technical, have produced the most destructive batsman in the game's history.

T20's gain has been Test cricket's loss, however. In 2009, six months after the tour to England, Gayle and the West Indies arrived in Australia for a three-Test tour to contest the Frank Worrell Trophy. The tour started miserably: Gayle was soon making a return journey to the Caribbean to care for his mother, who had fallen seriously ill; Ramnaresh Sarwan ricked his back and was ruled out of the first game; Jerome Taylor arrived and was clearly unfit. Gayle was back in the fold by the time the First Test rolled around, but the Windies were abject, beaten in three days, by an innings and 65 runs. The second game at Adelaide was a different affair. The West Indies eked out a 12-run lead in the first innings, before Gayle dropped anchor and became the first Windies captain to carry his bat in a Test innings. His final total, of 165 not out, came from 285 deliveries and took over seven hours. Had the innings come from Rahul Dravid or Shivnarine Chanderpaul, it would not have been so revered; from Gayle it amounted to a supreme display of self-control. The *Wisden* match report questioned his decision to bat into the last day for a lead of 329, but acknowledged that, following nine consecutive Test defeats against Australia, a draw was a victory of sorts.

The final Test in Perth was a study in contrasts, showcasing the variety that only Test cricket can offer. Australia's first innings score of 520 appeared to have smothered any hopes of the West Indies' gaining the win they required to level the series. Gayle evidently disagreed, and laid into the Australians, emboldened by the famous Perth bounce and quick outfield. For 72 deliveries he flayed the ball to all parts of the ground, with one blow recorded by *Wisden* as landing "on the roof of the five-storey Lillee-Marsh Stand a full 110 metres away". He scored at exactly a run a minute and, after 102 of them, he was spent, holing out to the fielder at point. In the time he took to score a century, the bewildered Travis Dowlin at the other end had managed just 31. It was the sixth-fastest Test century ever, and the third-quickest by a West Indian.[2]

Following Gayle's heroics in Australia, however, and in light of his stratospheric rise within T20, he played just eight of the West Indies' next 24 Tests. Gayle and the WICB tell contrasting stories about why they fell out in early 2011. Gayle claims that he was affronted by the board's failure to notify him personally that he had been dropped for ODI and T20 series against Pakistan; the WICB argues that Gayle had decided to play in the IPL and that it was unable to pick him. The issue is clouded further by a lack of clarity over his fitness. What happened since has had profound consequences for cricket: Gayle got his break in T20 and set about redefining the art of batting in the shortest game, while the West Indies have limped along, winning just two of the 16 matches they played without him. The feud was ended in time for the West Indies' Test tour to New Zealand in July 2012, and the team managed a creditable 2-0 series win. But a precedent has now been set: Gayle will play when and where he chooses, and is likely to continue to prioritise the IPL, the Big Bash, the Bangladesh Premier League, the Sri Lanka Premier League and the forthcoming Caribbean Premier League ahead of playing Tests for the West Indies. The effect on Test cricket has been saddening. As recent results show, his withdrawal has robbed the Test arena of a competitive team, while the reputation of one of its most iconic batsmen is now up for debate. I asked Gideon Haigh how he considered Gayle, having watched him score his contrasting hundreds in Australia, and he replied: "I just can't tell if he is a good

---

2   *The balance of power in the match continued to see-saw. After a West Indian batting collapse left Australia with a lead of 208, the home side were then bowled out for just 150. Chasing 359 to win, a century stand by Brendan Nash and Narsingh Deonarine threatened to get them over the line, but they eventually fell 35 runs short.*

player any more. I just can't tell how good Chris Gayle is. And I'm disappointed about that."

Gayle is the first man to fulfil the career path that was outlined by Andrew Flintoff in 2009, when the talismanic Englishman rejected the offer of a limited-overs contract from the ECB in order to operate as a free agent on the T20 gravy train. However, Flintoff's failure to recover from a knee operation meant that only after Gayle's divorce from the WICB did the concept of an international-calibre freelance cricketer become a reality. The appeal of going freelance to high-profile veterans such as Flintoff and Gayle is not hard to grasp. These men had spent a decade travelling around the world, turning out to play when they were told to. They were apart from their young families for months at a time. Five-day Tests are punishing on bodies that have been continually patched up. The launch of the IPL meant that the money on offer from national boards was put in a new perspective. They can now make a series of short appearances in T20 matches, with the freedom to pick and choose when and where to play, where there are plenty of keen young colleagues to field in the more demanding positions, where it is more important to score quickly than stay in, and where they won't have to bowl more than four overs. It is an exciting and lucrative final flourish at the end of a career.

But, if the IPL were simply a pension for ageing Test cricketers, there would not be the same concern about its effect on the five-day game. Rather, its attraction extends beyond that, appealing also to the young, talented prospects that it is hoped will become the next generation of Test cricketers. The teenagers of today have grown up not only with the elegance of Michael Vaughan's cover drive, but also the eponymous Tillakaratne Dilshan's *dilscoop*. One was a familiar sight in the restrained eminence of Lord's; other at the wild, carnival thrill-ride of the IPL. The links between cricket and Bollywood, the whispered rumours of debauchery at the after-parties, the contracts with extra zeroes, the capturing of the zeitgeist—the IPL, and T20 as a whole, is designed to appeal to the young. And who would fall harder for it than youngsters who play, as well as watch?

In an essay on life as a county cricketer, Martin Speight describes the career path for a young cricketer in England: "Once they have played at school or for a club's colt team, they end up playing club cricket or have trials for county under-age teams. Some progress through the county colts to the young cricketers (under-19s) and the best cricketers are given the opportunity to play county 2nd XI and then first-class cricket. It's a natural progression." For the very best, this journey, which allows a gradual accumulation of skills and a steady increase in commitment, has been abandoned in favour of the disproportionate financial rewards of T20.

Previously, players in their late teens learned how to lengthen the game of cricket. The former Indian Test opener, Aakash Chopra, writes: "Our growing-up years were all about knowing where the off stump was; learning about proper weight transfer, to keep the shots on the ground; and getting the defence impenetrable. Bowlers were taught the art of taking wickets in the longer format. Fast bowlers would regularly bowl with a ball that was 50–60 overs old, to develop reverse swing, while spinners would be encouraged to flight and turn it, and to acquire deception." It is a view confirmed by Malcolm Knox, who grew up playing cricket in Australia. "We didn't play a two-day game until we were about 18, it was all limited-overs cricket. But it isn't hit-and-giggle cricket when you're a kid, as 50 overs is a really long time. We played 60-over a side games from about 16; before that it was 30 overs."

The rise of T20 works against this process by encouraging young cricketers to shorten the length of the game that they play, before they have experienced much, if any, first-class cricket. Inevitably, the skills that they focus on are those that are recognised in the short game—clearing the ropes, scoring in every degree of the wagon-wheel and bowling a variety of deliveries. The goal for those that do it best is an IPL contract. And there is no doubt that the IPL is recruiting: franchises are incentivised to scout for young talent. International players can only be signed at the annual player auction, and recognised talent attracts high bids; not so uncapped players, who can be hoovered up at any time during the year. Four of the Indian squad for the 2012 Under-19 World Cup were already in possession of IPL contracts; the youngest, Vijay Zol, signed his contract with Royal Challengers Bangalore aged just 17. Reflecting on the appeal of T20 to young players, Rahul Dravid said: "There is no all-consuming desperation for them [India's young players] like there was for me and my generation to do well in Test cricket.

First-class and Test cricket were the only cricket we had. Today, there are more opportunities. I wonder what a 14/15/16-year-old today is thinking. I wonder what's going to happen five years ahead."

Dravid's quandary is the central question around which this chapter revolves. The burgeoning careers of two players relatively new to the Test arena offer very different views. David Warner, a stocky left-handed batsman, caused a minor sensation in 2009 when he became the first player to represent Australia without having played a first-class match, when he was picked for a T20 game against South Africa. That he scored a match-winning 89 from 43 balls was one in the eye for those that were troubled by the apparent selectorial disregard of the first-class toil that had always preceded international recognition. Those soothsayers who predicted Warner's lack of experience would be exposed in the five-day game have also been caught out. He scored his first Test century in his fourth innings, carrying his bat as Australia subsided to a seven-run defeat against New Zealand. He later gave a glimpse of the more familiar side of his game, clubbing 180 runs from 159 balls against India in Perth. His success raises interesting questions, particularly of those dismissive of T20. Warner has shown little difficulty in adapting his style of play in his infant five-day career. The discipline he showed against New Zealand suggested that it is possible for T20 players to succeed in Tests. Except it wasn't Warner's master-blasting against South Africa that caught the eye of the Test selectors, as Knox explains:

"Obviously, people had identified Warner's skill in short-form cricket, but he always looked like an orthodox player. He didn't look like a limited batsman. He was picked in the Test team on the strength of an innings he played in Zimbabwe on an Australia A tour, where he scored a double-century in something like 450 minutes. It was the first time that anybody had seen him play an innings of that length. He didn't score especially quickly. It was an Alastair Cook-type of an innings."

For the chair of Australia's selection committee, John Inverarity, Warner was a player of big potential and sound technique, who was ready to make the leap into Test match cricket. He was not chosen because of a perceived need to add impetus to the batting line-up. There was no call for big-hitting; he was simply the next man in line to replace the injured Shane Watson. It is still too soon to know what Warner represents. It is possible that he could become the first great Test batsman to have made his name in T20. Whether that is because of what he learned playing limited-overs cricket would be difficult to prove or disprove. It may be that he succeeded in the first instance at T20 simply because it offered him an opportunity earlier in his career. Or, he may prove to be a flash-in-the-pan. On his first trip to the subcontinent, he averaged 24 as Australia were whitewashed by India in four Tests, but there are many examples of Test batsmen who needed time to find their feet abroad. On his own, Warner is not a big enough sample for any conclusions to be drawn.

The development of India's Suresh Raina, by contrast, is a more useful case study, because his career has been that bit longer. Although he is exactly a month younger than Warner, he is considerably more experienced at international level. Like Warner, it feels like he emerged as a limited-overs batsman who then found his way into the Test team, rather than vice versa. His first ODI was back in 2005, when he was just 18, and his debut for the national T20 team was less than 18 months later. He had to wait until 2010, however, for his first taste of Test cricket. In the five years between his ODI and Test match bows, he established himself as a superb limited-overs middle-order batsman and fielder. The number of runs he made in that period (2,379) is not flattered by the number of caps that he won (98), but this reflects the fact that he tended to bat at six or seven. He faced an average of just 33 balls per innings in that period. More significant is his strike rate: 89.73. His role in the Indian one-day side has been to find gaps in the field and push the run rate up. Occasionally, if those above him failed, he was required to bat more circumspectly to rescue the innings—most notably against England in 2006 and Sri Lanka in 2010—but he has become India's finisher at the end of the innings.

His role in the Test team is less well defined, partly because he has been less successful. Apologists would argue that there are few tasks more thankless than being an Indian Test batsman of Raina's generation, as he and his contemporaries will never scale the heights of their forebears. Batting alongside Dravid, Tendulkar and Laxman will not generate favourable comparisons for many. As the junior batsman alongside the above trio, plus Virender Sehwag and Gautam Gambhir, Raina has frequently filled in wherever he has been needed, most often at five, a place higher than he bats in the ODI team. He made a bright start to his Test career, with a century in his first innings and two fifties and 41 not out in the next three, although his debut ton was made on a disgracefully flat wicket in Colombo, which only saw 17 wickets fall in five days. After the run-soaked tour to Sri Lanka, Raina began to struggle, averaging just 22 in his next 13 matches. By the end of the series in England in 2011, his confidence was shot, and he was dropped from the Test team for a year.

Much has been made of a perceived weakness against short-pitched fast bowling. Against England in particular he looked uncomfortable when James Anderson, Stuart Broad or Tim Bresnan banged it in short; this was exploited mercilessly, with Andrew Strauss setting a field with five slips, a gully and a close catcher on either side. In the second Test at Trent Bridge, his mind already frazzled, he top-edged a ball from Bresnan to long leg for a five-ball 1. Yet, as Raina himself has pointed out, his struggles in England were as much against the offspin of Graeme Swann, who captured his wicket four times out of eight, as against Anderson and Broad.

The reason for the failure of Raina's Test career to take flight lies in two separate imbalances: one technical, the other mental. His five years of playing international limited-overs cricket meant that he was a familiar face by the time he made his Test debut, and was even considered an experienced player. Yet, in reality, he was nothing of the sort. At the time of writing, almost three years on from his first Test, he has played only 81 first-class matches, compared with 170 domestic and international T20 games and 159 ODIs. When it comes to playing the sort of cricket required in Test matches, he remains extremely green. Years of playing limited-overs cricket meant that he was unable to defend for any length of time against Swann; similarly, players also do not receive the same criticism for mistiming a hook in the short games as they would in a Test because of the pressing need to keep the run rate up.

The editor of *Wisden India*, Dileep Premachandran, has identified Raina's deceptive immaturity, and compares his cricket education with his near-contemporary, Alastair Cook. The differences are interesting. Cook has played just 34 domestic and international T20s and 64 ODIs, but 182 first-class games. It is of little surprise that

Cook has enjoyed a much more successful Test career, as he was that much better prepared for it. However, Cook is also England's ODI captain, and, since he took on the 50-over leadership, has averaged over 50 in the format. Cook has been able to adapt his Test game to limited-overs more easily than Raina has been able to do the reverse, because Test and first-class cricket is that much more demanding. Early in his career, Cook had a problem when it came to nibbling outside off stump at balls on a full length, a tendency that saw him tormented by Stuart Clark in Australia in the 2006/07 Ashes. The unforgiving nature of Test cricket meant that he had no choice but to iron out his technique. Limited-overs cricket has been more generous to Raina. The late Peter Roebuck put it concisely and correctly: "Proper batsmen master a method and then adapt to conditions. It is much easier to go down than up, to go from five days to 20 overs."

The second imbalance relates to incentives. For Cook, there can be few higher planes to reach than the 766 runs he scored in seven extraordinary innings in Australia in 2010/11. He made big scores away from home under the most intense pressure, and in an environment where he had previously been found wanting. It is also still accepted in the cricket cultures of England and Australia that Ashes Tests are the stiffest examination of all. But would an equivalent number of runs for Raina in England in 2011 have had the same significance? In the age of the short game, I'd say not. Raina is most admired in India for his crucial stand with Yuvraj Singh in the 2011 World Cup quarter-final, which saw India beat Australia. It was an important knock, but it did not win the tournament for the team. Nevertheless, this is the extent to which the short forms matter in the cricketing nation of the future. I asked Gideon Haigh whether Raina could ever succeed as a top-class Test match batsman. He looked doubtful and said, "Mentally, he may not have the motivation. There is certainly no commercial imperative on Raina to learn how to play the moving ball. He won't play in England that often in his career. Money has chased him, rather than the other way around. He hasn't really had to go and look for it."

This is the anxiety behind Rahul Dravid's quandary, the other side of the coin from David Warner's breezy excellence. Raina and his generation have little incentive to excel at Test cricket. They can be adored by the fans and made richer than they ever imagined, without ever coming to terms with the format that makes cricket what it is. This is why supporters of Test cricket should be concerned about T20. It is not that fellow Test fans will get bored and look elsewhere; Tests have been enthralling crowds for over a century. It is lack of motivation for players to continue to strive for excellence. How many 14 or 15-year-olds will aspire to emulate Dravid's concentration and resilience, and how many Gayle's 150-metre six? Duncan Hamilton put it nicely, when he wrote, "An actor who only aspires to a part in a soap opera, and entirely styles his career towards achieving it, will never act beyond his range". This is his portrait of the T20 cricketer: comfortable, well-fed, limited. Imagine that player. Now imagine Test cricket played by 22 of them.

In the introduction to this book, I insisted that I was not advocating the abolition of T20. That remains the case, not least because, in addition to the financial support that it can add to a precarious profession, it would be myopic to ignore the innovation and excitement that it has brought to Test cricket. But, for all of these positive influences, the rewards are currently tilted too far towards T20, at the expense of the Test match. It is no use criticising the players for bailing out of national duty to head for the IPL when there is such a disparity in wages. Likewise, it is no good castigating boards for dismal attendances when Test teams are missing their star players.

The measures that could be taken to initiate a gentle reordering of the game are not drastic. They are more a collection of nudges in the right direction. They need not scare off the administrators, even such a timid organisation as the ICC. The first step, agreed upon almost unanimously by the players, administrators, journalists and officials that I have spoken to, is for the ICC to grant the IPL a window in its Future Tours Programme (FTP), the giant fixture calendar for international cricket. For the time being, the IPL is a permanent resident in the cricket landscape, and, therefore, it should be treated as such. The Test match has gained nothing from the ICC pretending that the IPL does not exist. As the IPL in its current form runs for seven weeks, from early April to late May, the greatest impact of such a move would be felt by the West Indies and Sri Lanka, as their domestic seasons would have to begin several weeks earlier, or be made several matches shorter. This is regretful, but surely it is more dignified than the sight of players deserting their countries *en masse* for India as the season builds to a climax.

The ICC has so far declined to offer a window to the IPL. Its objection is that a window would represent a concession of territory to T20 that may never be won back; if the IPL were granted a window, the Big Bash would demand one, and so would the Bangladesh Premier League. If either of these leagues survives to become the equal of the IPL, then they probably ought to have windows too. But there is little reason to believe that they will. Granting the IPL a window would also have another purpose, of course: it would offer some resistance against the tournament getting longer. It would be better for the ICC to make the IPL an official part of the cricket calendar than to allow it to continue to grow, unsanctioned, as a quasi-rebel movement. For this reason, the BCCI is unlikely to be impressed by this proposal, as not only would it limit the length of the tournament as it stands at present, it would also work against the long-anticipated expansion of the IPL to include a second tournament later in the year in a second country, such as South Africa. Given the ICC's lack of jurisdiction over the BCCI and the lack of incentives for the BCCI to co-operate, the prospects of an official window, for all of its merits, are slim.

Encouragingly, however, several of the most credible ideas to rebalance long and short-form cricket have come from India. Aakash Chopra has proposed bringing parity between earnings in the IPL and the Ranji Trophy, on the grounds that, "At present, the gulf is so huge that anyone in his right mind would happily sacrifice his first-class career to be a part of the IPL". If such blatant market distortions feel uncomfortable, it is worth remembering how far the IPL has drifted from its free-market principles. Chopra concedes that a ceiling at the IPL players' auction would spoil the drama of an event that has become an integral part of the IPL routine. His solution is to allow franchises to bid as much as they like, but for any fee above a certain threshold to be paid back to the IPL, rather than the player. On the first-class front, he advises that, rather than lift the salaries of all 500 players who compete in the Trophy, the top 20 bowlers, batsmen and all-rounders could receive IPL-level wages through a bonus system. These are nothing more than tweaks, but would prompt India's young players to give a second thought to first-class cricket.

Dileep Premachandran concluded his essay on Suresh Raina with a more ambitious plan: more A team tours, particularly to unfamiliar climes. As a possible measure to improve the quality of Test match cricket, it is a superb idea. The more time that Raina spends having to fend off the short ball, the more he would be pestered into correcting the flaw in his technique, or, as Harsha Bhogle argues, "Ishant Sharma would have become a better bowler, Virat Kohli a better batsman, if they had spent a month and a half playing in England. Apart from their cricket, they would have learned to look after themselves and handle responsibility." Ironing out basic technical errors among emerging players ought to mean smoother transitions when these players graduate to the Test team, and a more competitive set of Test matches. Dileep's ambition lies in persuading these players to take part, and the national boards to pay to play them. Those nations most committed to Test cricket do this already. In the summer before the 2011 Ashes, the Australian A team were in the ideal place, doing exactly the right thing: playing first-class cricket against the England Lions and English counties. But the BCCI is ambivalent (even "strongly opposed", in Bhogle's words) to its players going on A tours or signing short-term first-class contracts abroad. The players, too, might need some encouragement. When the next generation of Indian and West Indian cricketers are increasingly turning down the chance to appear in Test matches in search of a bigger payday elsewhere, travelling halfway around the world to play in alien conditions in front of a handful of local fans won't generate a queue at the airport. Nevertheless, the sight of India's A team touring the West Indies and New Zealand in 2012 was an encouraging one.

The best, and bravest, idea to come out of India, or anywhere else, has already been implemented. Following India's capitulation to Australia in the Border-Gavaskar Trophy, the team's second successive foreign whitewash, the Punjab Cricket Association (PCA) announced that it was to ban its under-21 players from T20 matches, including the IPL. The secretary of the PCA, MP Pandove said: "We strongly felt that 17-21 are the formative years for any player and there should be no distraction. The step which we have taken is in the larger interest of players and the country's cricket as a whole." A man with a foot in both camps, as assistant coach of Kings XI Punjab in the IPL and the coach of the Punjabi Ranji Trophy team, Vikram Rathour, echoed Peter Roebuck when he added, "I always believe that it is possible that a good player in the long format will be able to switch to the shorter format, but it doesn't always happen the other way around." It was a tacit admission that Suresh Raina's short-ball woes won't be solved in T20, but a few more years of first-class grind might just manage it. While these sorts of foresighted and altruistic decisions are being made, there is a chance that the current and next generation of Test cricketers might come to emulate their heroes.

To most, it feels as if the battle for the affections of today's teenage cricketers is in its infancy. After all, T20 is less than a decade old and the Test match is a centenarian. However, a 15-year-old in 2013 was just five when T20 was first played in England. Quite conceivably, it might be the only cricket that he or she has ever seen. Test cricket cannot afford a decade of mediocrity before it reaches out to young players and fans again. As this chapter has shown, the incentives for players are so heavily weighted in favour of T20 that the Test match in its current state of health may not survive that long. Since he made T20 his priority in 2009, there has been relatively little for Chris Gayle to regret. His success is also persuading other players to follow him. If the Test match is going to thrive again, these cricketers have to be given a reason to think twice.

Chapter Three

The Technology

"It is impossible to design a system so perfect that no one needs to be good."

TS Eliot

. . . .

Tucked away at the back of the Marylebone Cricket Club (MCC) museum at Lord's in London's leafy St John's Wood is a modern facsimile of a document written in spidery handwriting in 1727. On it are the "Articles of Agreement" between the Duke of Richmond and a Mr Brodrick, later identified as Alan Brodrick, Lord Middleton of Peper Harow in Surrey. The two gentlemen each commanded a cricket team—the Duke's was assembled from the staff on his estate—that were to play two matches against each other that year. Given the vast sums of money that were wagered on the results of these games, the men had the foresight (or perhaps had learned from painful experience) that it would be wise to draw up a list of rules to prevent the proceedings from descending into chaos. According to one historian: "Country house cricket was not known for its gentility. Four years after his game against Mr Brodrick, the Duke of Richmond and his team were attacked by a mob at Richmond because they arrived late and then wasted time, so that their cricketing and gambling opponents did not have a chance to win... The Duke, his team and his umpires were lucky to escape with their lives."

Of the 16 articles agreed by the Duke and Mr Brodrick, the 11th states: "That there shall be one umpire of each side; & that if any of the gamesters [players] shall speak or give their opinion on any point of the game, they are to be turned out; & voided in the match; this does not extend to the Duke of Richmond and Mr Brodrick."

This note established the balance of power on the cricket field, with players subject to the authority of the umpires and supplicant to their decisions. When the MCC, or the Cricket Club at St Mary-le-Bone as it was then known, first drew up its laws of cricket 60 years later, it preserved the Duke's position on umpiring. The umpires, the document states, "are the sole judges of fair and unfair play, and all disputes shall be determined by them; each at their own wicket". Despite the fact that the laws have since undergone two centuries of modernisation, the first clause on umpiring has been preserved verbatim. This means that, for the entire time that cricket has existed as a codified sport, the decision of the umpires has been final; it is the men in white who have provided clarity in moments of ambiguity.

There are several reasons why the authority of the umpires has endured. The first is boring and practical: the game only works if everyone plays to the same rules—and the umpires are best placed to ensure players comply. Similarly, players have chosen to accept umpiring decisions to ensure that the game does not disintegrate in the manner that the Duke feared. But the real reason why umpires matter is because they instil the values of the sport. As far as the meaning of cricket is concerned, they are the keepers of the flame. When a bowler thuds the ball into a batsman's pads, swings his body through a half turn, holds his arms aloft and beseeches an umpire to raise his finger, he looks like a man possessed. If the appeal is turned down, he will stalk back to his mark, disappointed, angry, but nonetheless will still submit himself to the umpire's ruling. Likewise, the batsman who feels the ball whizz past the outside edge of his bat and into the wicketkeeper's gloves, but looks up aghast to see the umpire giving him out, might rant and rave, but will still walk off the field as a show of respect. These situations—and each of us who has stepped onto a cricket field has experienced them—remind us of the importance of accepting a decision made in good faith, whether we agree with it or not.

The early rules employed such a draconian stance on the behaviour of players because Richmond and Brodrick understood not only that sport produces moments of conjecture and ambiguity, but also that the arbiters of the game are just as fallible as the players. Batsmen play at balls they should leave and leave balls they should play; fielders drop catches; and umpires give players 'out' when they should be 'not out' and vice versa. The most famous umpire of them all, Harold "Dickie" Bird, wrote in his memoirs: "We are dealing with inches and fractions of seconds and are bound to fall into error at some time or another. What is important to realise, however, is that umpires all over the world are honest men doing their best in difficult circumstances, without fear or favour."

And this fallibility has been no impediment to the development of the game. It was only as recently as 2002 that it was decided that both umpires in a given Test match had to hail from neutral countries, such had been the unstinting faith in the officials. However, in the past decade, the fact that Test match umpires make mistakes has suddenly become much less acceptable. It has been identified by players and administrators as a problem. Commissions have been launched to investigate it; and several solutions have been trialled to solve it.

There are two reasons for why we now demand perfect decision-making. The sport has become more professional, which is a covert way of saying there is more money riding on it. Higher revenue from broadcasters and more corporate sponsorship has been spent on facilities and staff to bring cricket more into line with rugby or football. The England and Wales Cricket Board (ECB), flush with revenue from Sky, describes how it has poured money into hiring a team of physiotherapists to keep the best players in top condition, employing fielding coaches to improve athleticism and has dispatched the England Lions (formerly England A) around the world to better prepare promising young players for five-day cricket. When England ascended to become the world's top-ranked Test team in 2011, it was, according to *The Guardian*'s Barney Ronay, "a case of familiar talent brilliantly managed. There will be other Ian Bells, other Stuart Broads: English cricket has always produced these players. What is different now is how thrummingly well conditioned they are."

And, so the logic goes, once the team is prepared and performing well, and grounds have been equipped with the latest technology available to ensure a desirable playing surface, why would boards not reconsider the role of the umpires, the men who, let's not forget, have ultimate authority over proceedings? Are they not another factor, like player conditioning and the state of the wicket, which can be brought under greater control? In recent years, cricket administrators have committed themselves to this train of thought, but without thinking enough about where it leads. As long ago as 2000, Christopher Martin-Jenkins remarked that, "Traditional sportsmanship often seems to be under threat from the exaggerated aggression of those playing the game for increasingly high financial stakes." It was a timely warning that has been almost entirely ignored.

Alongside a general trend for greater investment in cricket were the events of October 16 1998, which saw the sale of domestic broadcasting rights by the ECB to Channel 4, which broke the monopoly enjoyed by the BBC since 1938. It was a significant moment, likened by the former *Wisden* editor, Matthew Engel, to a second marriage. English cricket "…said farewell to the children's mother because she had grown crotchety and unglamorous, and climbed into bed with a sexy young frippet". Channel 4 appeared "sexy" because, as a novice at screening live cricket, it realised the need to bring innovation and imagination to its coverage. Matches were shown through more cameras and angles than ever before. The commentary team blended the comparative youth and vigour of Mark Nicholas with the technical expertise of Simon Hughes, known universally as The Analyst, and the experience of the much-loved Richie Benaud. There was a heavy spend on marketing, and, by creating an event around the cricket, under the banners of the Caribbean and Indian Summers, it made the sport feel both more accessible and part of something bigger than itself.

However, among the cricket fraternity, Channel 4 remains best known for the technological tools that it introduced to cricket broadcasting: the Red Zone, the Snickometer and Hawk-Eye. These tools were designed to be accessories to the experience of watching the game, as well as a way for the commentary team to mull over key passages of play. They turned out to have a much wider effect on the sport than anyone expected.

The introduction of Hawk-Eye tapped into a growing source of unease about how cricket and technology were interacting. An incident that took place in the Test between England and South Africa at Newlands in 1996 highlighted the tension. To the naked eye, it looked as if England batsman, Graham Thorpe, was well short of his ground when attempting to complete a run, but the square-leg umpire, Dave Orchard, said he was not out, and felt sure enough of his decision not to call on the third umpire, who was sat in a box with a television. However, the replays, which were shown in most of the hospitality boxes around the ground, showed that he should have been on his way. The crowd began to protest, as did the home team, with the captain, Hansie Cronje, calling first for the third umpire's opinion, and then for Thorpe to walk. After a consultation between Orchard and the other on-field umpire, Steve Randell, the view of the third umpire was sought and the original decision was overruled. The episode caused a minor uproar, with some accusing the South Africans of not playing fairly, while others argued that it was wrong for the player to remain on the field when so many in the crowd knew that the decision was incorrect. In his report on the incident for *The Times*, Alan Lee cut to the quick:

"This was an instance of a dismissal—and a crucial one—being imposed on an unwilling umpire by the ever more manipulative hand of television. Without TV replays, or even with no substantial crowd, Thorpe would not have been given out. This would have been an injustice, of course, but it would have been a decision taken by an umpire, in whom such power has always been invested, rather than one brought about by influences outside of the running of the game."

It was moments like this made the use of Hawk-Eye so attractive for broadcasters, as it meant viewers were as well, if not better informed, than the players, umpires and spectators about what had just happened on the field. Hawk-Eye is a tracking system that uses multiple cameras to follow the position and direction of a ball and translates them into an image. Using the information generated by the cameras, it can also be used to predict what the future path of the ball will be. This is what appealed to Channel 4, who saw that it could be used to adjudicate on lbw decisions. Hawk-Eye gives three pieces of information on lbws to the broadcaster, all of which the umpire considers when making his decision. The first is where the ball pitches (if the batsman is playing a shot, the ball must not pitch outside leg stump for him to be given out); the second is how high the ball is likely to have bounced (the umpire will be considering whether or not the ball hits the batsman too high up to go on to hit the stumps); and, lastly, the direction in which the ball would have been likely to travel had it not hit the batsman. This suddenly gave cricket audiences the chance to see, quickly and unambiguously, if a decision was right. Hawk-Eye proved to be one of the channel's most-loved innovations, and was soon also used to monitor the service line in tennis, where the line judge's decisions are similarly split-second and crucial.

However, Hawk-Eye also created a problem for the cricket authorities. Television was proving that umpires were sometimes wrong. We always knew they made mistakes, of course, but Hawk-Eye gave seemingly definitive proof one way or the other. Before Hawk-Eye, there was such a thing as a marginal decision—a call that was so close that the umpire's verdict was generally accepted.

These would be fought over for hours in the stands and pubs, but fans knew that there was no right answer; it was just part of the game. Hawk-Eye got rid of that by providing an answer in most instances. And without giving umpires the benefit of the doubt about those marginal decisions, it gave the impression that a lot more of their calls were wrong. The mood around umpiring changed; the certainty of the decisions began to ebb away. Players used growing doubt about umpires' abilities to appeal more often, in the hope of getting a dodgy decision. Eventually, there emerged a consensus that something had to be done about it. And, in 2008, under the weight of a more professional and expensive game, and an embarrassing disconnection between the game played on the field and the one watched at home on television, something was.

The Umpire Decision Review System—now known universally as the DRS—made its official debut in a series between New Zealand and Pakistan in 2009. It is a suite of tools available to the third umpire in the stands. It works something like this: suppose the fielding side appeals for an edge that is caught behind, but the appeal is turned down by the on-field umpires. Under the DRS, the fielding side can appeal the decision to the third umpire. The third umpire would then watch a video replay to determine that the bowler's delivery was legal. Assuming it was, he would call on a thermal imaging camera, known as Hot Spot, which shows any contact between the bat and the ball as a white spot or patch on the screen. If the replays and Hot Spot fail to offer him sufficient clarity, he can report back to the on-field umpires that the findings were inconclusive and the original decision would stand.

For the most difficult decisions of all, lbw appeals, the DRS comprises a pitch map, to show where the ball has pitched, and Hawk-Eye. The guidelines on the DRS produced by the International Cricket Council (ICC) advise that the third umpire should give a decision to the on-field umpires within 30 seconds of the referral. The combination of fast work by the third umpire and the efficacy of the technology is intended to ensure that decisions are made correctly, but without slowing the pace of the game.

Now, in 2013, five years of Test cricket have been played under the DRS. In that time, it has become clear that the DRS has failed in its brief of ensuring that umpiring decisions are made correctly, quickly and without controversy. Indeed, it is impossible to conceive of a decline in umpiring standards so great that it could have generated as much newspaper copy as has the DRS. *The Guardian*'s cricket correspondent, and former England Test player, Mike Selvey, was moved to describe the DRS as "taking over the minds of the cricket world, as if the game were scripted by Stephen King". Intended to soothe occasional outrage, it has produced no small amount of horror of its own.

The past five years of DRS-assisted Test cricket has helped us ascertain four facts. First, the idea that technology is able to remove ambiguity from umpiring is a fallacy. Second, the indications provided by the DRS need interpretation, and this interpretation has created a new source of umpiring error. Third, as humans are naturally incredulous, we have swapped our doubts about human judgement to disbelief that machines can be entirely accurate. Fourth, as Selvey suggests, the DRS has had a multitude of unintended consequences that have changed cricket far more than its designers intended.

Let us take these points in turn. There are many examples that suggest that the DRS does not always provide clarity and that it has failed to remove the umpiring howler from the cricket lexicon.[1] But the proceedings in the Third Test between Pakistan and England in January 2012 showed that the DRS also introduces confusion where previously there was none. In England's first innings, Abdur Rehman removed Kevin Pietersen lbw. On first viewing, it looked like a marginal decision by the umpire, Simon Taufel. Pietersen had shuffled across to leg, so that he was showing one-and-a-half stumps. He had also managed a small step forward, and the ball hit him just above the knee-roll. The batsman probably felt confident that the ball was going down the leg side and might have been too high. He reviewed the decision straight away. Hawk-Eye estimated that the height wasn't an issue, and that the ball would have just kissed the leg stump on its way past. The brush of the ball may not have been firm enough to dislodge the bails. Nevertheless, Pietersen was on his way. Yet, in the same innings, Saeed Ajmal appealed for another

---

1   *For those that argue in favour of the DRS on the grounds that it cuts out howlers, it would be worth pointing out that, if decisions were really that obvious, Hot Spot, HawkEye and the rest wouldn't be required. The only technology needed would be a bog-standard video replay.*

lbw decision, this time against Graeme Swann. The other umpire, Steve Davis, shook his head, so Ajmal sent the decision upstairs to the third umpire. This time, Hawk-Eye showed that much more of the ball was hitting the stump than in the Pietersen review, but not enough to have the decision overturned, so Swann was safe.[2]

This situation was particularly unsatisfactory because it implied that you can be both in and out to the same ball, a state of affairs that did not exist before the DRS. There is a technical reason why Pietersen was out and Swann was in, and it is because of the so-called umpire's call ruling. Hawk-Eye's developers acknowledge that the system has a margin for error, taken to be up to 25mm at present, in assessing where the centre of the ball will be when it reaches the stumps. This means that, on occasions where the middle of the ball is not inside the outer edge of the wicket by 45mm, the system rules that the decision is marginal. In these cases, the on-field umpire's original ruling takes precedence. In both the Pietersen and Swann examples given above, the ball was adjudged not to be sufficiently close to the stumps for the DRS to offer an accurate verdict. So in this match, the DRS offered nothing more than a closer look at Taufel's and Davis' decisions, which told us only what we already knew: that Taufel was more inclined than Davis to give a marginal decision as out. We were no closer to reaching a "correct" decision.

Six months after Pietersen was given out in Dubai, the South African all-rounder, Jacques Kallis, illustrated the second fact about the DRS, by becoming a victim of the umpire's inability to interpret the messages that the review system was feeding him. Kallis had scored three in the first innings of the Third Test between South Africa and England at Lord's, when the England bowler, Steven Finn, appealed for a catch behind the wicket on the leg side. Kumar Dharmasena turned it down, but England chose to review. The review showed that England were right—Hot Spot showed a mark where the ball hit Kallis' glove—but the third umpire, Rod Tucker, missed the fact that the batsman's hand was off the bat at the time. Tucker told Dharmasena that there was contact, the decision was overturned, and Kallis was given out. He shook his head all the way back to the pavilion.

---

2   *This example was first used by Mike Selvey in his article published in The Guardian, 'DRS is a friend to nobody'.*

The DRS did not malfunction at that moment—it gave the umpires all of the information that they needed to rule that Kallis was not out. But, perhaps because of the extra processes involved, the time pressure, his excitement at spotting the jump in the wave-form and the opportunity to right a perceived wrong, Tucker was unable to process all of the information that the DRS fed him, and he dropped a clanger. And—this is the crucial point—the incident demonstrated that the DRS has created an avenue for umpiring errors that had never existed previously. Had England not been able to review the decision, replays would have showed that Dharmasena's original decision was right (albeit perhaps for the wrong reasons). This is why it is wrong to consider the DRS, or any form of technology, as the Holy Grail. Technology can produce high-quality pictures, sound and video, but those media still require interpretation through the prism of the laws of cricket, and this interpretation will always remain fallible.[3]

Taking the DRS to heart has also seemed to mean surrendering part of our belief in the unpredictability of the game, and this has proven difficult to do on both an emotional and a logical level. Sport is often at its most engaging when feats that seem to defy the laws of nature take place. Who would have thought that a punk kid from Victoria could turn a ball four feet at Old Trafford, as Shane Warne did? Or that a youngster from Rawalpindi could propel a delivery at 100mph like Shoaib Akhtar? The use of the DRS suggests not only that these feats are possible, but that they are measurable by technology. By making that admission, we are all falling a little bit out of love with cricket.

Often, this emotional resistance is expressed as dissatisfaction with the technology itself, the third point outlined above. Most cricketers or commentators have a pet anecdote to use against the DRS. For the former England player and Test umpire, Peter Willey, it

---

3   Another example of this, which is too ironic to be ignored, concerns the former South African wicketkeeper, Dave Richardson. Unlike Graham Thorpe, Richardson did make his ground when an appeal was made in a one-day match against Pakistan in October 1994, but it was still referred upstairs to the third umpire, Atiq Khan. To the surprise of many in the crowd, and even more on television, Khan gave him out. He later confessed that he pressed the right button, but that the red, rather than green, light came on. The source of the irony is that it is the same Dave Richardson who, in his role as chief executive of the ICC, has guided the DRS into law and remains its greatest champion.

was officiating in a Test between England and Pakistan in 2001, just after the advent of Hawk-Eye: "I gave Alec Stewart out lbw. He was back on his wicket and the ball hit him on the pad, six inches above his foot. Shoaib Akhtar was bowling and Hawk-Eye had the ball taking off at an impossible angle, hitting right at the top of the stumps. But the ball only had a foot and a half to travel! It was going to hit half-way up at most. Everybody agreed it was absolute rubbish." For MS Dhoni, the Indian captain, it is believed to be an lbw appeal against Ian Bell in the 2011 World Cup. The appeal was turned down because the batsman was too far down the pitch for Hawk-Eye to measure accurately. ("I think the adulteration of technology with human intention was the reason why we didn't get that wicket", he said.)

Of course, there is so much cricket played that even a system that is almost always accurate will still generate the odd example that can be used to criticise it, and, taken individually, these incidents are relatively easy to dismiss. After all, nobody will remember the thousand occasions when Hawk-Eye showed the ball behaving just as everyone expected.

What is more difficult to deny is that the physics of cricket are sometimes just plain weird, and it is very hard to imagine that this weirdness can be simulated by a computer. As Gideon Haigh said to me, "If you've played cricket, the idea that the ball moves in straight lines according to computer predictions... it just doesn't seem to make sense, especially in England where the ball wobbles around so much". This is also the official reason why the Board of Control for Cricket in India (BCCI) refuses to sanction the use of the DRS in its Test matches. The BCCI president, N Srinivasan, has said simply, "We welcome technology when it is 100% error free. In this case, it is not, so we will continue to oppose [it]." The ICC and Hawk-Eye have gone to great lengths to reassure players, fans and administrators of the accuracy of the ball-tracking system—most recently commissioning independent research from a Cambridge University academic—but success in the science lab does not feel like a guarantee against future controversies on the field.

Of the four facts outlined above, it is the last that is the most important. Whether the DRS eventually removes every mistake from umpiring or not, its legacy is unlikely to be anything to do with officiating the game. Its major effects on cricket have actually been entirely separate from the problem that it was introduced to solve; a classic example of the law of unintended consequences. Who at the ICC considered that the introduction of a review system for umpiring decisions would lead to a resurgence in bat play, the re-emergence of slow left-arm spin, a dramatic improvement in on-field behaviour, or that a wedge would be driven between the BCCI and the rest? The answer is, of course, nobody, yet each of these things has become apparent since the launch of the DRS. The rest of this chapter will show how the ICC's chief executive, Dave Richardson, let slip the mother of all understatements when he told *Cricinfo* in 2012, "I think, if we're totally honest, the DRS has affected the game slightly more than we thought it would."

The first incontrovertible unforeseen benefit of the DRS has been the effect that it has had on batting. In 1957 Colin Cowdrey and Peter May neutralised the West Indian spinners, Sonny Ramadhin and Alf Valentine, at Edgbaston by thrusting their left pads at every ball that pitched outside off stump on their way to a legendary partnership of 411. This tactic revolutionised the way that batsmen played spinners. They recognised that umpires were naturally conservative when giving lbw decisions, and so were quick to get down the wicket to Ramadhin, in particular, so that the contact between ball and pad was well outside the line and a long way away from the stumps. Such was the advantage gleaned by batsman from this tactic that the lbw law was revised so that batsman could be given out if they were hit outside of the line when not playing a shot. Even so, umpires remained reluctant to give the benefit of any doubt to the bowler because they were given so little time by batsmen to read the direction of the ball after it had pitched.

However, the DRS has changed all of this. Hawk-Eye's ball-tracking technology has showed umpires what would (or at least might) happen to these deliveries if they hadn't been padded away—and a great many would have gone on to hit the stumps. As a result, umpires have adapted their behaviour, as Daryl Harper explains:

"I probably do give more lbws because of Hawk-Eye than I did ten years ago. My personal feeling is that the ball hitting the leg stump a decade back would very rarely be given out lbw because of the feeling that the ball was sliding down leg. But now we've seen so many times from the replays that the ball hits leg stump very often, and we give it not out much more than [the ones hitting] off stump. I've subconsciously made that adjustment. I wouldn't say I have become bolder, but more accurate. I normally store the Hawk-Eye situation, and use that bank of information along with little details like the bounce, the pitches, and use that to make the right decision in the field."

Umpires' new-found willingness to give lbw decisions has put the onus back onto batsmen. The panic that has set in was most clearly demonstrated by England—never the most comfortable team against spin—during their series against Pakistan in early 2012, when the team were defeated as much by their own uncertainty regarding use of the DRS as by the bowling of Ajmal and Rehman, contriving to produce a series of horrible dismissals. To be truly safe against finger spin in the DRS age, batsmen have to learn how to pick the spin and bring their bat into play, rather than lunging forward and smothering the ball without knowing which way it will turn. That a higher standard of batting is being demanded is a good thing, particularly after a decade in which technique has frequently been sacrificed in favour of faster scoring.

Unsurprisingly, some members of the batsmen's union are unhappy. Pietersen said during that tour, "In my career so far, this is the toughest I've ever found it. Batters are not getting the benefit of the doubt any more. Umpires are giving a lot more lbws. It just has to be clipping and you're out. Two, three, four years ago, you were never, ever out. I have had to change my game." Whether batsmen should ever have had the benefit of the doubt is an interesting point, and views tend to be coloured by where you stand in the batting line-up. Umpires' previous conservatism is understandable: batsmen are only out once, whereas the next lbw appeal could happen with the next ball. In other words, disappointing the bowler carries less risk than disappointing the batsman.

Mike Selvey goes against the grain, however, as a "spear-carrier" who contends that, after a decade in which the evolution of the game has firmly favoured the batsmen—the 2000s were nothing if not a time of bigger bats, flatter pitches and shorter boundaries—the DRS has swung the balance too far in favour of bowlers. He supports the argument that the margin for error in Hawk-Eye has seen "the stumps effectively widened by a ball width either side and one in height", and that this has given the bowlers more to aim at. In his full-throated defence of the DRS, Dave Richardson sees the rebalancing of the game in favour of bowlers as a good thing: "A year ago, every Tom, Dick and Harry was averaging more than 50 in Test cricket. That balance between bat and ball had got out of kilter. I think that using DRS may help to redress that balance." The sentiment is right, and forcing batsmen to use the piece of wood in their hands is almost always a good thing, but to claim it as justification for the DRS is disingenuous. The merits of the system should be judged purely against its brief, rather than its unintended consequences.

If life has become more perilous for batsmen, then the beneficiaries have been spinners, and particularly the least-heralded breed of slow bowler, the left-arm orthodox. Left-arm spin has rarely been a glamorous occupation, usually employed as a defensive move. "Tie up an end", "keep the run rate down", "get through a few overs", are instructions typically given by a captain to his left-arm spinner. And, among the crowd, the arrival of left-arm spin often seems to coincide with a bout of cramp or the sudden need for another trip to the bar. Put simply, finger spin is less highly rated than wrist spin because bowlers are able to put fewer revolutions on the ball. The champagne moments of spin bowling, where a ball moves two feet to beat the batsman, tend to come from wrist spin. However, what the DRS has done is bring finger spin, and in particular left-arm orthodox spin, back into the game.

Again, this is to do with umpires becoming more willing to give lbw decisions, and, ironically, the reason that left-arm orthodox spinners are becoming more successful is because they spin the ball less, which makes it easier for the umpires to figure out the trajectory of the ball. The stats appear to back this up. In the case of Rangana Herath, the Sri Lankan left-arm spinner, in the first six years of his international career, 19% of his Test wickets were taken lbw, but this has risen to 34% in the years since the introduction of the DRS. Abdur Rehman didn't even take a Test wicket lbw prior to the DRS, but, since then, they have accounted for more than one-third of his dismissals. Poor old Ashley Giles, who was almost always used by England as a defensive bowler, will be cursing his luck that his Test career ended just before the advent of the DRS: less than 14% of his Test wickets were lbw. Had be been playing now, his tally of 143 Test wickets would be closer to 200. No wonder Kevin Pietersen, no stranger to being undone by a slow left-armer, described such bowlers as "gold dust".

And it isn't only left-arm finger spinners that are benefiting—the DRS years have coincided, or perhaps encouraged, off-spinners too. Saeed Ajmal, probably the best spinner in contemporary Test cricket, was helped along to becoming the fastest Pakistani to 100 Test wickets by collecting 36 lbws. By contrast, just nine of the first 100 wickets taken by the most prolific off-spinner of them all, Muttiah Muralitharan, were lbws. Or, for a contrast between life before and after the advent of DRS, consider the difference in the role of Graeme Swann in the England team to that of Giles. Swann is there not only to tie up an end, but to take wickets and break partnerships. Statistics, at least, argue that the main reason for this is that Swann bowls in the age of the DRS, whereas Giles did not.[4] In his history of spin bowling, Amol Rajan noted that Swann has taken a startlingly higher percentage of his Test wickets lbw compared to other England off-spinners. As of May 2013, 27% of Swann's Test dismissals were lbw, compared with those of John Emburey (10.9%), Peter Such (10.8%) and Robert Croft (16.3%). Again, the obvious reason for this is the change in umpiring brought about by technology.

The DRS has also changed the behaviour of the players. When I asked umpires and players about the effects of more technology on cricket, I quickly found myself in a discussion about the reduction in appealing, rather than about decisions being made correctly. This is another of the DRS's unintended consequences. The president of MCC, Mike Griffith, put it as follows: "Players can now be made to look extremely stupid if they are seen to be making mischievous appeals. My old county, Sussex, when Mushtaq [Ahmed] was

---

4   There may also be a case that Swann's effervescent personality demands that he be used in this way. He is too frothy a character to be content with as defensive a role as that of Giles.

playing, appealed at times incessantly, putting the umpire under great pressure." Sussex, of course, was far from alone in committing this offence on the ears. For Gideon Haigh, "You soon see when it comes to reviewing which ones a player thinks are out and which ones they are just trying it on for."

The DRS acts as a disincentive to over-appealing in two ways. First, it essentially calls the bluff of the fielding team. If an umpire shakes his head, it can put its money where its mouth is, and contest the decision, which it will only do—and risk losing one of its two reviews—if it feels there is a genuine chance of the decision being overturned. Second, the only reason for appealing endlessly is the hope that the umpire will be pressured into feeling that one of the many appeals must be out. But, with the DRS, if the batsman feels that this is the case, he can review the decision. If it was indeed made as a result of the umpire growing weary, or being pressured, it can be overturned. There can be little argument that this is anything but a good thing, but, again, it was not in the DRS mandate.

There is a case to be made, too, for the introduction of technology having improved players' all-round conduct. Mike Atherton has noted that the number of cricketers found guilty under the ICC's Code of Conduct has fallen steeply in the past few years. The ICC maintains a list of infringements of the code dating back to its introduction in 1992 on its website (perhaps to ensure that those who transgress are not easily allowed to forget their misdemeanours). It can be an interesting read when the referees are colourful in their descriptions or write up incidents hardly worthy of the name. Are we really to believe that Phil Tufnell brought the game into disrepute "by throwing the ball in aggressive manner after caught behind appeal turned down" during a warm-up game against Australia A in 1994? Although there does not seem to be any reduction in the number of breaches recorded in recent years, fewer and fewer of those that are recorded take place in Test matches, and more in Twenty20 (T20) and one-day internationals (ODIs).

The DRS would seem to be a logical reason for this, not because there are no longer any incorrect umpiring decisions for players to rail at—dissent over umpiring decisions (along with, boringly, wearing incorrect kit) has been the most common infraction reported—but because it is less satisfying to rage against the machine than against a man in a white coat. There is also a sense of the decision being referred to a higher, less tangible power, when it is sent 'upstairs' to the third umpire, which means that players have no obvious target for their invective. This is a double-edged sword for umpires: most will be grateful for improved player behaviour, but there is a concurrent loss of authority.

Atherton is also wise to point out that "poor umpiring begat poor behaviour". Perhaps inevitably, given the authority vested in them, umpires have always been a cause of player dissent. David Fraser notes that, while the first-ever Test match, between Australia and England in Melbourne in 1877, passed off peacefully, an England tour a year later saw the captain of New South Wales refusing to play unless England replaced an umpire who had given a debatable decision in favour of the tourists. The situation was inflamed by the enormous amount of money staked on the result by those in the audience, and soon the English captain, Lord Harris, was surrounded by a rioting mob on the pitch. Disputes about the quality of the umpiring on both sides has been a feature of Test series' between England and Pakistan since the early 1960s and continued right up to the Pakistanis' 2006 tour of England, when Darrell Hair and Billy Doctrove suspected the tourists of ball-tampering. Steps have gradually been taken to try to diffuse this sort of row, with the introduction of the ICC elite umpiring panel and umpires from neutral countries. But it is the DRS that seems finally to have put sufficient distance between angry players and the source of their frustration. Naturally, the ICC has been quick to claim this as another victory for the DRS—Dave Richardson, yes, him again, noted, following an ICC meeting in 2012, that "The DRS has almost totally eradicated player dissent." Never mind that the DRS was set up for a different reason entirely.

A fourth entirely unintended consequence of the DRS is the wedge that has been driven between the BCCI and the rest of the cricket world. No one outside of the BCCI can be certain why the Indian body took against the DRS when it did or why it has maintained its opposition so vociferously. For now, the more strongly that the ICC advocates the DRS the more adamantly the BCCI is compelled to reject it. What we do know is that India and Sri Lanka were the guinea pigs of the first iteration of the DRS when it was trialled in a Test series in 2008. It is fair to say that the Sri Lankans made a better fist of using the new tool. They made 11 successful referrals; India, by contrast, made just one. Interestingly, in that series, which Sri Lanka won by two Tests to one, the winning team's trump card was an off-spinner, Ajantha Mendis, who bowled a sackful of variations. Mendis took 26 Indian wickets in that series—his first in Test cricket—bowling the line and length that led Rajan to describe him as "An ultra-modern bowler, somebody who has fundamentally conditioned his style to take advantage of umpires' increasing willingness to give batsmen out leg-before." Sri Lanka were streets ahead in terms of understanding the technology and its potential, while at least part of India's residual opposition stems from their miserable experience at Mendis' streetwise hands.

One particular incident sticks in the mind. In the First Test in the series, the Indian captain, Anil Kumble, padded up to a ball from Mendis, which then looped into the hands of the fielder at silly point. The umpire gave Kumble out, but it wasn't immediately clear whether he was out lbw or caught. In the confusion, Kumble decided to review it; the review confirmed that he was plumb lbw, but that it wasn't clear whether the catch was clean. Kumble remained out, but there was uncertainty whether the reason had been shifted from the catch to leg-before. It didn't necessarily matter, and it certainly wasn't a turning point in the match, but it typified India's disgruntlement with the new rules that they still have not come to terms with.

Does it matter that the BCCI refuses to accept the DRS? Unfortunately, yes. It is not conducive to the best Test cricket for some matches to be played according to one set of rules and some to another. And, as I have attempted to demonstrate, the DRS has stealthily grown to affect far more than the "problem" it was designed to solve, which makes its uneven use more problematic. Gideon Haigh gave me a good example: "There was the ridiculous situation where 2011's Australia-New Zealand Test matches used DRS and then the subsequent Australia-India series did not. Michael Hussey was given out on review to a borderline lbw in the second innings at Bellerive for 0 [against New Zealand], and the next Test match, at the Melbourne Cricket Ground (MCG), he missed his first ball by six inches, was given out and couldn't review it. So, he was undone by the inconsistent application of technology."

By setting the bar at 100% accuracy, the BCCI does not need many examples to show that the DRS is falling short. And the ICC is probably pursuing the wrong strategy by attempting to verify its accuracy, because, as we have seen, the errors are often errors of interpretation as much as issues with the technology. And, in the fact that the BCCI is generally impervious to ICC pressure, it appears that the current, unhappy situation is likely to continue for some time to come.

My final observation on the effects of the DRS is the decisive one for many commentators, including yours, and it is this: it robs cricket of its spontaneity. This is a particularly grievous loss, because the moments of drama are so staccato and unpredictable. A sensationalist example, but imagine the end of the Edgbaston Test in the 2005 Ashes in the age of the DRS. With three runs needed for a remarkable come-from-behind Australian victory, Steve Harmison bowls, the ball brushes Michael Kasprowicz's glove and Geraint Jones takes a tumbling catch. But the England celebrations, so joyous and deranged in reality, are stilted and tepid. Kasprowicz takes the only option available to him: he uses his team's last remaining review. He and Brett Lee meet in the middle of the wicket. The England players stand around, hands on hips, the fate of the Test, the series, *the whole cricketing summer,* depend on the adjudication of the third umpire in the box. Eventually, he spots that Kasprowicz's hand was off the bat when the ball hit the glove. The decision is overturned. Pandemonium is postponed. Kasprowicz returns to the crease; Harmison trudges back to his mark. The decision is correct, accurate. But knowing what we know, is that really a preferable outcome?

An extreme case, perhaps. But, routinely, it now requires the sight of stumps cartwheeling down towards fine leg before we know for sure if a wicket has been taken. (And, even then, depending on the status of the batsman, he might review it just in case it was a no ball.) And in a sport that sometimes lacks for action, curtailing those moments in search of perfect justice seems perverse.

In fact, much about the DRS is strange. It is odd that an issue that would not have registered among most spectators' concerns about Test cricket has come to dominate a decade of play, and transform so many previously unconnected areas of the sport. But there is no doubt that it is here to stay; technology is a genie that has been allowed to escape from its bottle.[5] As it continues to be applied to more and more areas of cricket, administrators would be wise to spare a thought for Richmond and Brodrick and their decision to invest umpires with the authority of the game. This is, piece by piece, being handed over to technology, which generates more accurate decisions, but does not result in great sport. To my mind, and to the majority of the players and fans I have spoken to, umpires are not yet anachronistic. But they soon will be if their authority continues to be hollowed out.

In the mid-1990s, when video replays first emerged and the audience for cricket on satellite television was growing, the left-wing firebrand and cricket fan, Mike Marqusee, wrote a satirical, dystopian short story on the Test match. In it, he described the following scene:

"About half way through the first session of play, I saw one of the rituals for which Lord's is famous. In Heritage Cricket they have real live umpires, one standing behind the stumps at the bowler's end and the other at square leg. At a certain, predetermined moment in the game, the umpires 'get it wrong'. This was always very popular and always included in the digi-cast highlights. Of course, just like in GladCric, all the decisions were really made by a computer network of electronic eyes.

The umpires were linked to the network by ear-pellets and simply carried out the computer's adjudications. I have to admit that it did make the game seem more human. I guess that's why they evolved the ritual of 'getting it wrong', to make the illusion of humanness more convincing. At a certain point, the computer was programmed to misinform the umpires so that they 'got it wrong'. I noticed that when this happened (two or three times a day) all the box-dwellers fell about in fits of self-satisfied laughter."

It feels quite close to the bone, doesn't it? There is no perfect resolution to the technology issue. Some, such as The Old Batsman, have proposed taking reviews away from players, but allowing

---

5   There are areas where technology has indisputably improved cricket. Replays for run-outs, for example, promote fielding excellence. Where umpires previously needed to see clear evidence that a batsman was out—which meant that some deserving instances of athletic fielding went unrewarded—video replays now show to within a split-second frame whether a batsman has made his ground.

umpires to use them when they see fit. The logic makes some sense, particularly as it would stop players using them as a tactical aid, but it would redouble the pressure from the players on the umpire, who would implore them first to give a decision and secondly to use the technology. It may also lend to an eventual decline in standards, if umpires gradually lose the courage of their convictions. Imagine a situation where the umpire, seeking to uphold his authority, makes an incorrect decision and refuses to consult the technology. We would be back where we were a decade ago. When I interviewed Peter Willey, I asked him whether Marqusee's dystopia could come to pass; he shook his head and gave me a sad smile. "Then who would hold the jumpers?" he asked.

Chapter Four
The Pitches

> *"The thing you worry about at night is the wicket...*
> *the whole thing depends on it."*
>
> *John Stephenson*
>
> ....

Imagine a dangerous pitch, one that could do real harm to the cricketers playing on it. The chances are it resembles the one that England encountered at Sabina Park in Jamaica in January 1998. Before play even began it looked a mess, the shiny surface broken up by deep cracks and patches of long grass. The pitch had been re-laid just weeks before, and it didn't appear to have held together. The West Indian opening bowlers, Courtney Walsh and Curtly Ambrose, were dangerous enough under normal circumstances to keep batsmen focused, but the alarmingly inconsistent bounce meant that run-scoring was relegated behind self-protection. Opening batsman, Alec Stewart, coped manfully with balls that shot through at shin height and others that flew up and over the wicketkeeper's head to the boundary. As fully occupied was the England physio, who, in less than an hour, made six trips to the middle to assess injured batsmen. The game was abandoned with 10 overs bowled and England wobbling at 17-3. It remains the only Test match to have been called off because of an unsafe pitch. Stewart later described it as "54 minutes of hell".

There have been plenty of other dangerous pitches, however, many of them in recent memory. How about the SSC in Colombo in 2010? Or Hyderabad in the same year? Karachi and Ahmedabad, both in 2009, are also contenders. And there are lots more. These pitches couldn't be more different from the Sabina Park strip, which carried the risk of serious physical harm. These were featherbeds, making batting a pleasure and bowling as much fun as sweeping the stands after the match. Collectively, these pitches are far more dangerous than one-offs like Jamaica. The cricket played on them only vaguely resembles the unyielding, competitive, anxious psychodrama of Test cricket at its best. There is no confrontation between batsman and bowler; everyone knows that the batsman will win. Instead, they become contests between teams of batsmen to see who can produce the most grotesque, supersized score. Without this personal duel, the match loses its intensity and drifts for hundreds of overs, while centuries and double-hundreds are chalked up. Such pitches are lulling Test matches into inertia, at a time when five-day cricket needs to show itself as hard and intense, not flabby and soporific.

The scorecards for these matches belong in their own hall of shame. Colombo in July 2010 may be the most ghastly of all. In their first innings, Sri Lanka racked up 642-4, with a double-century for Kumar Sangakkara and centuries for Mahela Jayawardene and Tharanga Paranavitana. India responded with 707 all out. Sachin Tendulkar scored 203, Suresh Raina 120 on debut and Virender Sehwag 99. Even the last three Indian wickets added 115. Sri Lanka spluttered to 129-3 at the close, before everyone was put out of their misery. Almost 1,500 runs were scored for the loss of 17 wickets. Tendulkar, showing why batsmen should never be trusted, described the pitch as "the best in the world". Incredibly, the same two teams had played an almost identical game less than a year before, in Ahmedabad. In that match India racked up 426 and 412-4, Sri Lanka 760 (including 275 for Jayawardene). If anything, the pitch became easier, not harder, to bat on as the game progressed.

The Test between India and New Zealand in Hyderabad in November 2010 was another draw, entirely untroubled by tension, with New Zealand able to make 448 on the fourth and fifth days to avoid defeat. Earlier in the game, Harbhajan Singh and Sreesanth combined to put on 105 for the tenth wicket during India's first innings. Rather than revel in his rare century, Harbhajan said the groundsman "deserves to be given the contract to build national highways". Karachi in 2009 was another tedious draw, this time between Pakistan and Sri Lanka. Jayawardene—again—and Thilan Samaraweera put on 437 for the fourth wicket as Sri Lanka racked up 644-7. Their hosts showed that this was a little below par by compiling 765-6. The Pakistani captain, Younis Khan, scored 313.

Nor is this a South Asian phenomenon. In the West Indies, lively pitches have followed the team's battery of fast bowlers into retirement. The Test as Kensington Oval in Bridgetown, Barbados in 2009 saw England score 600-6 and the home side reply with 749-9. There was still time for England to crawl to 279-2 in their second innings before everyone was allowed to go home. St John's in Antigua is another serial offender. In 2005 a farcical Test with South Africa ended in a predictable draw. Eight players in the match scored centuries. In the West Indian first innings of 747, made over 15 hours, all 11 South Africans had a bowl, presumably to keep them all awake. At the same ground in the previous year, Brian Lara had made his record score of 400 not out. England were forced to follow on after the Windies scored 751, but never looked in any danger of losing.

Of course, among the 2,000 Test matches that have been played, some high-scoring draws would be expected, just as there are a few wins by an innings and the odd game that is over in less than three days. But the past decade has seen more than its fair share of run-fests on flat decks. Of the 50 Tests with the highest number of runs scored per wicket, more than one-third have taken place since 2000, and one-fifth since the trend for dead surfaces really took off in 2005. There was never a finer time to be a Test match batsman than in the second half of the last decade. In 2009 the average number of runs per wicket soared to 37.8; the scoring rate to almost 3.4 an over. No fewer than 22 batsmen averaged over 50 with the bat that year, and all of them scored a minimum of 300 Test runs. Inevitably, this meant that some moderate batsmen were made to look positively Bradmanesque. Among the 22 were Ramnaresh Sarwan, Shane Watson and Phillip Hughes, none of whom you would want to bat for your life. Daniel Vettori, whose batting is no more than an occasional bonus to New Zealand, averaged 59.92, while 16 of the 22 averaged over 60.

Behind this avalanche of runs was the desire for what former England fast bowler, Steve Harmison, memorably described as "chief executive wickets". These are placid, slow tracks that hold together for the full five days; pitches that offer little pace or bounce to fast bowlers, fail to swing for seamers and do not crumble sufficiently to interest the spinners. They are squashed flat by the heavy roller and stripped bare of the grass that gives the ball zip. The wickets themselves are built with Ongar or Surrey loam, a soil that is "to pitches what Imodium is to diarrhoea", according to Stephen Bierley, permitting no disintegration or substantial wear.

To put them in context, these pitches are the result of a 50-year evolution that began with the decision to cover Test match strips in order to prevent the weather from interfering with play. Veterans of uncovered pitches tend to speak of the stronger technique that batsmen and bowlers had in that era; bowlers required wit and variation to exploit helpful conditions, batsmen needed patience and the ability to play straight to survive times of wildly varying bounce and exaggerated swing. (The fact that a greater proportion of innings were ended by freak dismissals is less widely discussed.) The decision to cover them up reflects the belief that pitches are no longer supposed to play an active role in the game. The factor with the greatest influence over the direction of the match, it now holds, should not be the pitch. There is some validity to this argument. Although greater exposure to the weather can enable some inventive captaincy, Test matches should not be hostages to fortune.[1] However, the mentality behind the decision to protect the pitch from the weather (and therefore the players from extreme conditions) has stuck. Pitches are now not permitted to possess much of an identity of their own, interfere with play, favour one side over the other, or change character abruptly. This is a modern phenomenon. There was no such thing as a typical Test match pitch, even as recently as 20 years ago. What you got depended on the continent, the country, the city and the conditions. Now, the slow, low, flat strip has become the pitch of the 21st century, and it isn't doing Test cricket any favours.

Harmison attributed these pitches to chief executives, because, if they benefit anyone, it is the sport's administrators. Flat pitches produce Test matches that fill the time—all 15 possible sessions—ensuring maximum ticket sales and the greatest amount of airtime to be sold to advertisers and broadcasters. Rights to show Test matches in India, which is now by far the most lucrative market, have been sold by the day, rather than by the match, which means that the state association hosting the game has a financial imperative to make Tests last longer.[2] A Test match that lasts until the evening of the third day will only generate 60% of its potential revenue. Whether the match is entertaining is, in financial terms, irrelevant.

Yet it is blindingly obvious that this logic is flawed. India's 2010

1   In the 1937 Ashes Don Bradman chose to reverse his batting order in Melbourne, after seeing England bowled out for 70 on a pitch that had been soaked by a storm. It worked a treat. Australia went from 97-5 to 564 all out as conditions improved, and won by 365 runs.
2   The deal struck by the Board of Control for Cricket in India (BCCI) and ESPN Star (now solely Star) covering domestic rights for 2012-18 was worth around US£500m; Sky paid around £280m for a deal covering international cricket in England over 2014-17.

tour of Sri Lanka saw play in 44 of 45 sessions, but was a wretched
advert for Test cricket. Sri Lanka Cricket (SLC) banked decent
broadcasting revenue for that series, as did the associations that own
the grounds, but the cricket did nothing to persuade spectators to
come back when India are next in town, or to attract young fans to
Test matches over Twenty20 (T20) or football. Firstly, the groundsman at the SSC in Colombo, Anuruddha Polonowita, attempted to
deny that the pitch had an effect on the match, asking journalists,
"Why are you talking about the pitch? Why don't you talk about the
bowling? Both sides have weak bowling, both sides have brilliant
batting." Both teams were stuffed with batsmen, but six of the Sri
Lankans weren't required to bat in either innings, despite the fact that
they were playing against an Indian attack that had taken over 450
Test wickets. The pitch would have neutered even the West Indian
quicks of the 1980s. Polonowita then changed tack and suggested
that the strip was created for the benefit of the spectators: "Why
do crowds pay and come? To see cricket. If you want it to finish in
three days, I can fix the pitch for three days. That's not cricket."
This is just fundamentally wrong. Crowds watch Test cricket to be
entertained; they do not buy a ticket to wear as a badge of honour.
And there can be no doubt that cricket is more exciting when the
result is in doubt. In Colombo it was obvious before lunch on the
third day—less than half-way through the match—that the game
would be drawn.

To give him the benefit of the doubt, Polonowita may have been
constrained in what he could say. The issue of whether groundsmen
are put under pressure by their employers to produce a certain kind
of wicket is a touchy one. It seems to be an open secret; something
that occurs regularly, but quietly. Peter Roebuck was convinced that
it happens, insisting that, "Putting pressure on groundsmen to roll
the guts out of the surface so that the match goes the distance has
done more harm than good." The Australian journalist, Malcolm
Conn, told me of his suspicions, but added, "I've never been able
to confirm it". Steve Rouse, the former groundsman at Edgbaston,
described to me how, "There wasn't a direct request [for flat pitches];
it was expected by chief executives. It was a must that the match
had to last for a minimum of four days. Jobs were on the line. If it
was over in three days, or two-and-a-half days, year after year after

year, you wouldn't stay in the job." The man responsible for over-seeing Test pitches for the sport's governing body, the International Cricket Council (ICC), Andy Atkinson, tells a similar tale: "When my first Test as a head groundsman was completed in the last over of the fourth day, the very next morning I was invited to join the CEO in his office, where he told me that, because my pitch did not produce five days' play, I had cost the club £150,000." Whether this was a friendly joke or a genuine threat depends on the tone of the conversation. If nothing else, it stuck in Atkinson's memory.

Pitches have a tendency to get under the skin of cricket's admin-istrators. The current Marylebone Cricket Club (MCC) president, Mike Griffith, recalled a conversation with the head of cricket at Lord's, John Stephenson, who told him, "The thing you worry about at night is the wicket. The most important thing in the whole of Lord's is the wicket. The whole thing depends on it." You don't get similar quotes in other sports. Football and rugby pitches are fairly uniform, and only tend to be discussed in the case of extreme weather, which top clubs have invested large sums of money to combat.

Test match cricket has more in common with tennis, where the differences in the surfaces determines what kind of shots can be played and the strategy required to win the match. Mastery of clay-court tennis can be roughly analogous to playing on slow, turning tracks on the subcontinent. The ball moves more slowly off the surface, reducing the chances of pure speed forcing a mistake from an opponent. This also means that there is greater emphasis on making the ball spin in order to deceive. The difference between these surfaces and the grass of Wimbledon or the seaming wicket at Headingley is so great that success on both demands a versatility that some players, no matter how talented, do not possess. Pete Sampras, until recently the most successful male tennis player in history, never won the French Open; Adam Gilchrist has an overall Test batting average of just under 48, but in India it is 28.5.

But where Test cricket differs from tennis (and limited-overs cricket), and what makes the pitch an even more important factor, is the length of the game. Understanding, or, more likely, guessing, how the pitch will change during the match is paramount in the mind of the captain when he wins the toss. In *The Art of Captaincy*, Mike Brearley recalled a particularly brave decision by Tony Greig:

"When we were discussing our policy during the team dinner on the night before the [1977] Centenary Test in Melbourne, [Bob] Willis' reaction to Greig's remark that he was seriously thinking of putting Australia in was that it would be 'sheer lunacy'... He afterwards admitted that Greig's decision was absolutely right—the pitch gradually assisted batsmen more the longer the match went on." The combined first innings scores were 233, the second 836. England still lost, by 45 runs, but Greig did at least manage to give his team the best of the conditions.

Misreading the pitch can also have dire consequences. For decades, Len Hutton's decision to put the Australians in at Brisbane in 1954 was the classic cautionary tale. "Never before had an England captain taken such a gamble in Australia," *Wisden* reported. The home side racked up 601-8; England made 190 and 257. Hutton did, however, have the excuse that the uncovered pitch was soaked not long into England's innings, changing its character entirely. Fifty years later, Nasser Hussain had no such excuse when he made the same choice at The Gabba—clearly a ground that does strange things to England captains—on the first morning of the 2002-03 Ashes. After a conversation with Marcus Trescothick in the nets, where the ball was moving in the air, he felt that England's best chance of gaining the upper hand was to take early wickets. As he recounted to *The Observer*, "The ball swung a bit at first and I thought: 'Maybe this is going to work out.' But, by the fifth or sixth over, nothing was happening and the world was closing in on me. I thought to myself: 'Oh God, Nass, what have you done?' " At the end of the first day, Australia were 364-2. England lost the game heavily and, soon after, the series. These examples emphasise the role that the pitch plays in the Test match; no England football captain has ever been blamed for a defeat because he chose the wrong end to kick from.

Because of the influential role that the pitch plays, it is crucial that good surfaces are prepared, in order to enable a contest between batsman and bowler to take place. Superficially, there appears to be a consensus on how a good pitch will behave. Ask a cricketer, administrator or journalist what a good pitch will do, and chances are the response will be similar. Here's former Kent, Middlesex and England batsman, Ed Smith: "Cricket is at its best when there is a balance [between bat and ball]." And Mike Griffith: "What we want is pace, bounce and the pitch deteriorating towards the end of the match, so that the spinners play their part." And Mike Brearley: "I admire those groundsmen who are prepared to take a chance by going for hard, dry bouncy pitches that favour fast bowlers and genuine spinners, and make more pronounced the gulf between class batsmen and the rest." And current Australian Test batsman, Ed Cowan: "I like my cricket being an even contest between bat and ball." And the Argus Report commissioned by Cricket Australia (CA): "Each pitch should offer a good balance between bat and ball. The toss should not be decisive." And, finally, former Sussex captain, John Barclay: "The 'best' surface is one that is going to, at some stage, help the batsmen, but good bowling can also be assisted."

The ICC issued its own guidelines for match referees in 2006, which look remarkably similar to the views above. The objective for groundsmen is to prepare a pitch that will "provide a balanced contest between bat and ball over the course of the match, allowing all the individual skills of the game to be demonstrated by the players at the various stages of the match". Accordingly, a pitch rated 'very good' by the referee should have good carry, limited seam movement and consistent bounce, little or no turn on the first two days, but should become more and more responsive to spin as the game progresses. Conversely, a poor pitch will exhibit "excessive" seam movement, unevenness of bounce, assistance to spinners, or little or no seam movement, or little or no bounce and carry. These rules look fairly unambiguous at first glance, but it is interesting that three of the four criteria for a poor pitch protect batsmen from bowler-friendly conditions, and only one militates against the slow, flat pitches that make bowling a chore.

The ICC requires referees to complete a pitch report at the end of each Test, assessing the grass coverage, moisture, use of the heavy roller and the extent of bounce, movement off the seam and turn. If a referee rates a pitch as 'poor' (as opposed to the lesser crime of being 'below average'), the host can be fined up to £10,000 and given a directive to improve the playing conditions. If the offence is the second within a five-year period, the fine is doubled. The national association may choose to withdraw the ground from the firing line for a period of time. There are stiffer penalties for strips such as Sabina Park in 1998, which cause the cancellation of fixtures.

The big contention with Test match pitches is that the unbalanced nature of ICC guidelines—where pitches that offer help to bowlers are considered more offensive than those that assist batsmen—is resulting in the wrong sort of pitches being prepared. Not a single Test match pitch has ever been reported to the ICC for offering too little assistance to bowlers. This sends an implicit signal to groundsmen about the kind of strips that should be prepared, and is tilting the sport away from the types of surface that produce the best matches.

Not one of the featherbed pitches identified above—Colombo, Hyderabad, Bridgetown, Karachi, Ahmedabad or St John's—was rated 'poor' by the match referee. The most recent pitch to have been deemed substandard by the ICC was at Galle, following a Test between Sri Lanka and Australia in September 2011. The match lasted into the second session of the fourth day. Australia won the toss and batted, making 273, built around a gritty 95 from Mike Hussey. Sri Lanka's first innings was a disaster, with the Australian offspinner, Nathan Lyon, taking 5-34 on debut. Australia replied with 210, giving Sri Lanka a notional chase of 379 to win. From the depths of 68-5, a partnership of 142 between Jayawardene and Angelo Mathews gave the hosts some hope, but they eventually subsided to 253 all out, with a seamer, Ryan Harris, taking 5-62.

The pitch was dry and spun from the first day. Michael Clarke, captaining Australia for the first time, said it was "one of the toughest wickets I've played Test cricket on" and suggested the state of the pitch meant that the game was won as soon as he called the toss correctly. The Sri Lankan captain in the match, Tillakeratne Dilshan, added that a dry pitch was usual in Galle, but that he was surprised that it turned from the first day. The ICC's general manager for cricket (now its chief executive), Dave Richardson, in a ruling that upheld the match referee's decision, noted that the pitch turned too much too soon and that the bounce was occasionally uneven. In adjudicating on pitches, too much attention is paid to batsmen complaining that scoring runs is difficult and too little to the competitiveness of the cricket. Runs, just like wickets, have to be earned; they should not just be bestowed by virtue of occupying the crease. There was no doubt that the Galle Test was competitive—Clarke praised his team for posting a good first-innings score. But, for all that the pitch deteriorated and the batsmen had to earn their runs, Jayawardene still managed to make the biggest score of the match, in the fourth innings. Conditions were far from unplayable, and made for a far more entertaining Test match than the run-fests seen 50 miles north in Colombo.

Of all the comments made by players on the Galle Test, there was a lone voice offering support for low-scoring, competitive matches, and it belonged not to a bowler, but to Australia's rookie opening batsman, Ed Cowan, who made his Test debut a few months later. In an essay for *Cricinfo*, Cowan refuted Clarke's assertion that the match was decided by the toss, and argued that the game showed off Test cricket at its best. "It is exhilarating seeing the ball nip about or kick out of the rough. A slight feeling always exists, deep inside, that your average may take a battering, but that also means runs will be cherished, and that there is a challenge to be risen to every ball. It tends to bring the best out in you." Clarke understood that really—he claimed that Mike Hussey's 95 was worth "at least 150 on that wicket"—but his membership of the batsmen's union meant that he refused to express a preference for testing wickets over flat ones. Given its batsman-friendly criteria for pitches, the ICC also fails to see the importance of lively wickets. The editor of *Wisden India*, Dileep Premachandran, wrote in 2009 that, "Somewhere along the way, we've allowed a particular mind-set to take root. A sporting pitch seems to have become a synonym for one that aids the pace bowlers." I would go further than this and say that a sporting pitch has become one that aids batsmen, and makes life difficult for bowlers of all actions.

Despite the often frosty relationship between national boards and the ICC, there is little hope of the former standing up to the latter on the issue, as they are already incentivised—through gate receipts—to prepare the flattest pitches that they can get away with. It is interesting that, when the most powerful and combative of the national cricket boards, the Board of Control for Cricket in India (BCCI), was warned by the ICC for the pitch used in a Test against South Africa in Kanpur in 2008, the response was meek compliance. The match scorecard doesn't immediately suggest that there was anything wrong with the pitch. The first innings scores of 265 and 325 were ideal, and wickets were taken by both spinners and seamers. In the third innings, the South African batting fell apart to be all out for 121, before India knocked off the required 64 at more than 4.5 runs an over. In truth, the pitch was extremely dry. The ball kicked up dust and blew the top off the surface when it landed, but *Wisden* laid the blame for the collapse not with the pitch, but with the tourists' collective mentality: "South Africa's batsmen responded strangely, almost in protest at having to play on such a surface, attempting to block their way out of trouble, rather than trying to put some runs on the board. The approach was never going to succeed with almost three days of play left, and merely hastened the end." They had been undone by a classic, old-fashioned Indian wicket, one that saw the jubilant home team reward the groundsman with a Rs10,000 (£100) tip.

However, the ICC match referee, Roshan Mahanama, was not amused, remarking that the pitch was too dry and that it turned considerably from the first day. The BCCI did not contest the warning, and its secretary insisted, "I can assure everyone we will take all steps necessary to ensure this does not happen in the future." The BCCI clearly took the warning to heart, because the pitch produced for Kanpur's next Test, against Sri Lanka a year later, was unrecognisable from its predecessor. India ended the first day on 417-2, the first time that India had ever scored more than 400 runs in a day. So shell-shocked were Sri Lanka that, in pursuit of an eventual Indian total of 642 all out, they lost by an innings. The Sri Lankan coach, Trevor Bayliss, mindful of the South Africa game, picked three spinners and a lone seamer, and found that his bowlers got no assistance on a slow, true surface. The ICC's intervention succeeded only in turning an interesting, challenging wicket, full of local character, into an utterly benign strip, so friendly to the batsmen that the opposition wilted quickly. If a Test was ever decided by the coin toss, it was not Galle 2011, as Michael Clarke had claimed, but Kanpur 2009.

The other matches on the 2008 South African tour of India also highlight the direct bearing of the ICC's guidelines on the pitches produced and the imbalance within the guidelines themselves. The First Test at Chennai could easily have been included among the rogues' gallery at the beginning of the chapter. According to *Wisden*, it was "destined to be a draw before a ball was bowled. The Chennai pitch, once firm and sporting, had played slow and low in recent years, and this one proved no different". South Africa won the toss, batted, and scored 540. India responded with 627 (319 of them scored by Virender Sehwag). The game continued to fester, until it was eventually ended with South Africa on 331-5 in their second innings. Despite an average of 60 runs per wicket, the match referee felt the pitch was of a sufficient standard. The second game, at Ahmedabad, was a curious one. South Africa won by an innings and 90 runs; India were skittled for 76 in 20 overs in the first innings, having chosen to bat. South Africa made an imposing 494-7, before bowling India out for a second time, for 328. The pitch was again at the heart of the match; *Wisden* reported that a hot summer had necessitated that a lot of grass be left on the top of the strip to keep it from falling apart. A distinct green tinge to the strip was ideal for the South African seamers, and the Indian batsman failed to cope with the sort of sideways movement reminiscent of Headingley, rather than the southern hemisphere. The South African coach, Mickey Arthur, reined in his reaction to the pitch, admitting only to being "surprised". He probably danced a jig around the outfield.

With this context in mind, it is much less surprising that the Kanpur pitch was so traditionally *Indian*. The hosts were 1-0 down in the series and needed a win. The groundsman earned his tip by preparing just the sort of track that India needed to maximise their chances of a win. The dusty surface (and the South Africans aversion to it) gave India a huge advantage in the match. The series also highlights the central issue on pitch preparation, which is the extent to which the home side has the right to produce a surface to suit itself. On this subject, the ICC guidelines turn a blind eye. Provided that the pitch complies with the minimum standards, it doesn't matter whether it is at The Wanderers, Wellington or Wankhede Stadium, or whether a strip plays to its reputation or changes from one game to the next. This is as it should be. It is not for the arbiters of the game to tell the Yorkshire committee that it must prepare Headingley so that it swings, or New South Wales that Sydney must spin. Consequently, India were able to prepare a slow, turning pitch at Kanpur; their only error was that the pitch was so dry that it attracted the attention of the match referee.

Nevertheless, if a home side is seen to derive some benefit from a pitch, or if the pitch is thought to have been doctored in some way, the tourists are certain to claim that skulduggery has taken place. Mike Brearley describes the "smooth transition" between attempts to produce a pacey, interesting pitch to "shadier efforts to favour one's own side, to downright cheating". Somewhere along this spectrum there is a line—invisible in the ICC code—that it is considered morally wrong to cross. Bill Gordon, the long-serving former groundsman at The Oval, became "the most notorious man in Australia since Ned Kelly", according to the ECB's Chris Wood, following the decisive Test of the 2009 Ashes. The series was tied at 1-1 after four Tests, but, as Australia had won the previous series, England needed a win at The Oval to take back the urn. The Oval, of course, has a reputation for being one of the best batting wickets in England, but batting out time would not have been enough for the hosts. In the days before the match, the chief executive of Surrey, Paul Sheldon, told the national press, "There will be no cooking the books just to produce something to England's advantage. The pitch will be a very fast, bouncy wicket with an even covering of grass. There will be a bit of life in it early on and it should spin a bit towards the end. But it will essentially be a batting wicket. Games often go to five days here, but you tend to have a result." Sheldon, of course, had other reasons to hope it would go the distance, but the Australians seemed to take him at his word. They dropped their offspinner, Nathan Hauritz, for the match, in favour of a four-man pace attack, supplemented by the part-time spin of Marcus North. England retained Graeme Swann.

After England completed victory, by 197 runs, the chairman of the Australian selectors, Andrew Hilditch, admitted that, "Everybody misread the wicket." The captain, Ricky Ponting, harrumphed, "I don't think anyone in their wildest dreams thought the wicket would play the way it did." The pitch was closer to a sub-continental track than an English greentop, turning from the opening day. England posted a competitive 332 in their first innings, before Australia slumped to 160 all out in theirs. Although Swann took 4-38, it was Stuart Broad that took out the top order, removing Shane Watson, Ponting, Mike Hussey, Michael Clarke and Brad Haddin, suggesting that there was plenty in the pitch for seam bowlers, too. England had a momentary wobble at the start of their second innings, which was precariously balanced at 39-3 at one stage, before eventually recovering to 373.

North's 4-98 from 30 overs hinted at the damage that Hauritz might have done. A defiant stand of 127 between Ponting and Hussey in Australia's second innings held England up, but Swann took another four wickets to seal the series. The Australian media piled into Gordon, describing the pitch as "dodgy", while Shane Warne said that the groundsman "over-baked" the pitch to ensure a result.

The Australians were also aggrieved at the pitch in Mumbai five years before, in a brief, but thrilling Test that India won in three days. After Clarke had taken an absurd 6-9 with his part-time slow left-armers, Australia needed just 107 to win in the fourth innings, but were undone by a five-for from Harbhajan Singh and were all out for 93. Ponting put the blame squarely on the shoulders of the groundsman, Polly Umrigar: "It's fair to say that the wicket was nowhere near even being close to Test-match standard, that's pretty obvious given what we've seen over the last two days. Forty wickets falling in just over two days of a Test is pretty much unheard of." There's no doubting that the pitch affected the game—Indian captain, Rahul Dravid, said it was "not ideal"—but, at both The Oval and Wankhede Stadium, Australia batted with ill discipline and lacked the temperament to adjust to the conditions. However, in these situations it is easier to hang the blame around the neck of the groundsman than to find deficiencies in your own dressing room.

There are, of course, occasions when neither the home team nor the groundsman can do much to influence how the wicket plays. The former New Zealand batsman and India coach, John Wright, tells this story about the Test that preceded Mumbai 2004:

"The venue was Nagpur, in central India, where the pitch was usually slow and low, a draw wicket as opposed to a result wicket. For this Test, it underwent a dramatic change that had nothing to do with global warming. There'd been a BCCI election narrowly won by the Jagmohan Dalmiya faction. The president of the host association in Nagpur belonged to the anti-Dalmiya faction. In the lead-up to the match, he was quoted as saying that the wicket was tailor-made for fast bowlers, and Glenn McGrath couldn't have asked for a better pitch for his 100th Test. I didn't really believe that the BCCI elections could have any bearing on a Test wicket until we got to Nagpur three days before the game and found that the local officials were permanently unavailable and even the groundsman wasn't talking to us... After the game, I asked umpire, David Shepherd, for his take on the wicket: 'John,' he said, 'it was as if they [Australia] prepared it for themselves.' A foreign journalist called it 'a 22-yard suicide note'."

In India, local politics trumps even the fate of the national cricket team. Despite India's controversial win in Mumbai, Australia won the series 2-1.

Neither side has it totally right on the home-advantage argument. On the one hand, Test match cricket is a bigger, more colourful and more interesting sport for the diversity of the pitches that it is played on. On the other hand, however, there is danger in arguing that the home side has the inalienable right to prepare the strip as it wishes. If unchecked, this will to win could easily see pitches become caricatures, so Indian or so English that spectators are denied a proper contest. Touring sides are already struggling to compete: the proportion of Test matches won by the home team has risen steadily from one-third in the 1980s to almost one-half in the 2000s. There are several possible reasons for this, including the reduction in the length of Test match tours and a decline in the number of players participating in first-class cricket abroad. For all of the evidence of flat pitches, the proportion of matches drawn has fallen over the same period, from around 40% to 25%, in inverse proportion to the rise in the average scoring rate. (The proportion of away wins has been relatively static.) The existence of ICC guidelines on pitch performance is justified by the fear that the proportion of home wins will rise further, even if the contents of the current laws are skewed against lively strips.

On the other side of the debate is the fear of over-regulation, of guidelines that become compulsory, leading to pitches playing the same the world over. In 2010 former Somerset batsman and journalist, the late Peter Roebuck decried the loss of identity that had occurred in Australia. Traditionally, a tour to Australia was one of the stiffest examinations of technique because each of the

Test pitches was distinct from the others. Brisbane swung on the first day and then became progressively easier (a reputation that did for Nasser Hussain); Perth was the quickest, bounciest pitch in the world; Sydney took spin early; Adelaide was one to bat on first. But, by the end of the last decade, these differences had disappeared: "Perth had become tame, the Gabba had lost its edge, Melbourne's drop-in pitch was sleepier than a teenager at breakfast time." Ed Smith noticed the same pattern in England, and elsewhere: "The idea was that a good wicket was a flat wicket and it had certain material characteristics, which then could be added to anywhere, any country. So wickets lost their local identity and became more of a central template, duller and more homogenous."

And then something changed. The *annus mirabilis* for batsmen, 2009, proved to be the peak (or trough) of this particular trend. There is no statistical measure to assess the state of Test match pitches, but those that correlate with flattening pitches—the number of runs per wicket and the number of runs per over—fell in 2010, 2011 and 2012. Aside from perennial hopeless cases, such as the SSC in Colombo (where the most recent Test, between Sri Lanka and Pakistan, saw first innings totals of 551-6 and 391), pitches appear to be moving further back towards the equilibrium between bat and ball. There may be reasons why runs have proved hard to come by, such as the introduction of the Decision Review System (DRS; see previous chapter) for umpires and the arrival of a new generation of fast bowlers, that have nothing to do with the pitches. Nevertheless, there have been more terrific Test matches in recent times, and some perilously low scores, which strongly suggests that pitches are being revived.

The extent to which this is deliberate is unclear. There has been no ICC diktat on the subject. In Australia, the Argus Report, commissioned by CA following the national team's impotent performance in the 2010/11 Ashes, found widespread dissatisfaction with the pitches used at domestic level, and recommended that each pitch should be "unique, depending on local soil, history and climatic conditions", to give first-class players experience of playing in different circumstances. The states accepted the line and ran with it, with no better example than the Bellerive Oval in Hobart.

Traditionally as flat as a pancake—Australia's average first-innings score in Tests there between 2000 and 2010 was 506—the pitch has since undergone a startling transformation. At the Test between Australia and New Zealand in 2011, possibly the most exciting that the two sides have ever played, all 40 wickets went down for less than 750 runs. The tourists bowled out the hosts, who were chasing 241 to win, for 233, amid desperate tension. On a pitch that was tinged with green, there were early wickets for fast bowlers (James Pattinson took 5-51 in New Zealand's first innings), turn for spinners (Nathan Lyon polished off the tourists' second innings with 3-25) and runs for batsmen who were prepared to bat with patience. David Warner's 123 not out in Australia's second innings was a landmark effort; one that "showed the mettle of the bloke", according to Malcolm Conn, and cemented his place as a Test match batsman. There was a bit too much swing for the game to be the perfect example of a balanced contest between bat and ball, but, after the indigestible run-feasts of previous years, it was a match to savour.

The story of the Bellerive wicket is worth telling in full, as, were it to be repeated around the world, the damage to Test cricket done by flat pitches would be healed in an instant. Mike Brearley argues that any team with ambitions of winning matches should prepare "result" pitches. He suggests that a decent team, playing at home, can expect to win twice as many matches as they lose. During a hypothetical 12-match season on a flat pitch, half of the games would be drawn, and, of the remaining six, Brearley's XI might win four and lose two. But, on a lively wicket, just two games would be drawn, and Brearley's team would win six and lose three. In a first-class league, this would leave them better off, and, therefore, a confident captain should support his team by asking the groundsman for a decent wicket. And this is what has happened at Bellerive.

For decades, first-class cricket proved elusive to Tasmania; the team was denied entrance into Australia's main competition, the Sheffield Shield, multiple times in the 1960s and 1970s, and, even when they were eventually allowed to participate in 1977, they were given a cut-down fixture list. Until the start of the 2009/10 Shield, it had won the competition just once. In that season, the Bellerive pitch played to expectations and Tasmania drew three of their five matches at home, winning only one. (Even that win was narrow, by one-wicket, against Western Australia, after scrambling 200 runs in the final session to beat the clock.) However, over the following winter, the curator, Marcus Pamplin, allowed the grass to grow and triggered a change in Tasmania's fortunes. In the following two seasons, the team won eight games out of 11 at Bellerive, winning the Shield for the second time in 2010/11, losing in the final in 2011/12. They also won it again in 2012/13. The matches themselves have also had a startlingly different complexion. In the five years before the pitch was reawakened, the average first-innings score at Bellerive was 304, a number that would have been considerably higher were it not for the fact that a decent proportion of those innings were declared. Over 2010/11-2011/12, this fell to 266, meaning that teams are now scoring, on average, 40 runs fewer per innings. The only variable that changed in this time was the pitch.[3] Tasmania's success in reaching the Shield final in both years shows both the truth behind Brearley's argument, and the kind of positivity lacking in Test cricket.

For the Tasmanian approach to catch on, two prevalent attitudes need to be overcome. The first is the pervasive wrongheadedness that says that lively first-class pitches will have a deleterious effect on Test cricket. Here's what Mike Hussey has to say about the return of interesting pitches to the Sheffield Shield:

"Certainly when I was growing up, the pitches were a lot truer and a lot better for batting, so, as a batsman, 1,000 runs [in a season] was a good benchmark and, if you got to that, you knew you'd had a good season. But I think that has certainly lowered in the last few years. I'm a bit concerned, to be honest. It seems like the nature of pitches around the country are really result-based. I'm concerned that batters aren't learning to bat for six hours and construct long innings and concentrate for long periods of time. I'm even concerned about preparing seam bowlers for Test cricket, because the margin for error is so big, they just have to lob the ball somewhere up there and it will do a fair bit and they're going to pick up their wickets. [But] in Test match cricket you've got to be very patient, very disciplined, for long periods of time. I'm a little bit concerned that we're not developing players and skills for Test match cricket."

---

3   *The relative strength or weakness of teams in the league should be cancelled out by the large number of matches included in the sample and the fact that Tasmania played each team every season.*

This is, on the whole, disingenuous nonsense. The technique and concentration of Australian Test batsmen will not be improved by batting for six hours on a featherbed and making 150. If anything, homogenous domestic conditions lull players into a false sense of security, which is dispelled when they encounter unfamiliar environments. If batting averages are in decline as a result of CA's edict to liven up pitches, it simply reflects the fact that the current generation of batsmen have spent too long playing uncompetitive cricket in overly friendly conditions. Four or five years of playing on a variety of challenging pitches is a much surer way of developing tough, technically correct cricketers to represent Australia in Test matches. Hussey's line on bowlers is also deficient. If we accept that cricket is a zero-sum game, where batsmen succeed when bowlers fail and vice versa, to argue that lively pitches give too much help to bowlers who only have to "lob it up" to get wickets, then it is to also admit that batsmen have had to do little to earn their runs on flat tracks. Hussey is showing his colours as a batsman. A man used to considering cricket from the popping crease has confused what is good for batsmen with what is good for Tests.

The second sticking point will be much harder to overcome, and that is the anxiety of administrators to maximise revenue from Test cricket by preparing flat wickets to ensure five days of play. When conducting interviews for this chapter, I heard frequent admissions that total attendances at Test matches would be higher if spectators were promised three and a half days of exciting cricket, rather than five days of monotonous run-scoring. To embrace this logic would require a national cricket board to accept that Test cricket's long-term future is more important than the revenue it generates in the short term. This would be a bold step, but undoubtedly the correct one. After all, three-fifths of something is more than five-fifths of nothing.

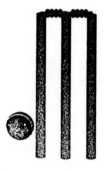

Chapter Five
The Fixers

> *"As the culture of a team can change rapidly,*
> *so can the culture of an entire sport."*
>
> *(Michael Atherton)*

....

After the first day of a Test against England at Supersport Park in Centurion in January 2000, South Africa were wobbling at 155-6. The start had been delayed and the evening curtailed by rain, meaning that only 45 overs were bowled. More rain and a sodden outfield meant that there was no further play on the second, third or fourth days. It was one of those occasions where a draw seemed such an inevitability that even turning up at the ground seemed a waste of time.

By the morning of the fifth day, the skies had cleared and the players were preparing to go through the motions when the South African captain, Hansie Cronje, approached the England wicketkeeper, Alec Stewart, on the stairs of the pavilion and made him an offer to keep the game alive. He said that he would declare South Africa's first innings and forfeit their second. In return, he suggested that England declare their first innings without a ball being bowled, and then attempt to chase down his team's first-innings target. Initially, the England captain, Nasser Hussain, turned down the opportunity. The pitch had been under the covers for three days and neither side was sure how it was going to play. However, after 45 minutes on the field (and having watched a hung-over Darren Gough bowl like a drain), Hussain was reassured. The South African middle order of Lance Klusener, Shaun Pollock and Mark Boucher batted sensibly and the pitch behaved itself. Hussain sent a message to Cronje that he was interested in a deal.

Cronje's first offer, of a total of 270 in 73 overs, was rejected. Undeterred, he made a second offer, of 255 in 73 overs. Hussain rejected that one, too. A third suggestion then came down, of 245 in 76 overs, which the England captain accepted. The South Africans scored a four from the last ball before the declaration to push the target up a little higher. Suddenly, a dead Test, one that was all but certain to peter out to a draw, was revived. To those in the crowd and following on television, and to the rest of the cricket world, it seemed a marvellous gesture; one that upheld the spirit of the game. England went out into the middle to push for the win, but found runs hard to come by. Michael Atherton went cheaply, and, although Mark Butcher and Hussain scored some runs, they came slowly. When Chris Adams fell to Nantie Hayward to leave England struggling on 102-4, Hussain would have been forgiven for thinking he had turned a certain draw into a defeat.

But a partnership of 126 between Michael Vaughan and Stewart saw England most of the way home, and when Gough hit a boundary to win the game with five balls remaining, the reaction outside the England dressing room was buoyant. A win had been created out of nothing. *Wisden* quoted the chairman of the England Management Advisory Committee, Brian Bolus, as saying that "sanity had prevailed"; too often in the past, Test match cricket had failed to show similar ingenuity to make the best of a situation. The South Africa coach, Bob Woolmer, also saw the bigger picture, suggesting "Hansie did the game the biggest favour imaginable at the dawn of the new century." And no less a figure than Christopher Martin-Jenkins proclaimed "Initiative and a sense of public responsibility triumphed over the kind of dog-in-the-manger attitude that sometimes gives cricket a bad name." Unfortunately, for once, CMJ was completely wrong.

Four months later, the truth about that day started to seep out. Cronje's behaviour did not quite add up. He had not hesitated to offer Hussain a second and third chance to make a game of the Test once the England captain had rejected his initial offer. Nor did he seem to mind risking South Africa's 14-match unbeaten streak, or upsetting his teammates. Klusener described himself as both "angry" and "a little bit astounded" at Cronje's plan to revive the game. On the field, too, Cronje appeared a little too keen for the game to reach a conclusion. Atherton described how, at one stage, Hussain sent down instructions to Vaughan and Stewart to bat out the draw, rather than risk losing further wickets. Cronje's response was to set attacking fields and give debutant all-rounder, Pieter Strydom, a bowl. Suddenly, the pressure relented, scoring runs became that little bit easier, and the chase was back on. (Cronje later claimed that he had no choice but to bowl Strydom, because of an injury to his other spinner, Paul Adams.)

What had happened was this: on the night of the fourth day of the Test, Cronje's phone rang. On the other end of the line was Marlon Aronstam, a man who worked for a bookmaker in South Africa and who gambled in his spare time. He knew enough about betting to realise that the wet weather had cut bookmakers' odds on a draw very short, and also, more interestingly, that he could get extremely long odds on either England or South Africa somehow winning the game. He realised that he could back both sides at long odds and cover himself by laying another bet on a draw at much shorter odds. It was a good plan, but only if a win for either side could be contrived.

Aronstam proposed to Cronje that, if the captain were able to produce a victory of any description, he, Aronstam, would donate a sum of money, variously remembered as 200,000 or 500,000 rand (£13,000 or £32,000) to charity. This led to a meeting at the South Africa team hotel, where the two discussed the different ways that money could be made on cricket matches. Cronje said that the co-operation of the players was required; Aronstam said that he would also be willing to pay for pitch reports and estimates of future scores from the captain. By the time that Aronstam left, a plan had been hatched for Cronje to engineer a result. In return, Cronje received two payments from Aronstam, totalling 53,000 rand (£3,400), although it remains unclear what proportion of the funds were paid for the Centurion fix, and how much was a sweetener for future dealings.

Despite the risk of appearing overly keen in his negotiations with Hussain, Cronje held his nerve and kept his end of the bargain almost perfectly. Although some players have since described how the outcome of the match made them uneasy, such feelings were not expressed publicly. Aronstam, however, did not fare so well; he ran out of time to get his bet on and ended up out of pocket. The only man to benefit from the fix, therefore, was Cronje. Even after the details of the deal were made public and his involvement with bookmakers was exposed, he maintained that, "The match delivered a genuine result and was in no way manipulated," However, this does not explain why a captain known for his caution and aversion to risk was so eager for Hussain to make a game of it, to the point where he was willing to risk losing the respect of his teammates. His argument that the spectators deserved a good day out is just not strong enough. The drama of that fifth day, which appeared to be so spontaneous and enjoyable, was entirely artificial.

Thirteen years on from Centurion, it feels like cricket is in the throes of a struggle against corruption every bit as epic as in cycling or athletics, and that its players have proved every bit as susceptible. The past two decades of international cricket have generated a lexicon of names and phrases synonymous with scandal and unfair play: "spot-fixing", "dirt in the pocket", "John the Bookmaker", Danish Kaneria, Hansie Cronje, Maurice Odumbe. A depressingly long list of players, from the best that the game has ever seen to the plainly mediocre, have dabbled with corrupt practices, some very deliberately, some unwillingly, and a few probably entirely by accident.

Yet the Centurion game remains the only proven example of a Test match where a player has been able to manipulate successfully the outcome for financial gain. There have been other Tests, such as England and Pakistan at Lord's in 2010, where we know that players received payment from a third party for bowling particular balls at a predetermined time, and others, such as that between Pakistan and Australia in Karachi in 1994, where we know that one corrupt player offered others money to underperform. But all that we have learned from these games is that some players are susceptible to corruption.

This information alone is not enough for us to assess the extent of cricket's problem with cheating. It does not tell us anything about how the mechanics of match-fixing work or whether it is possible to make money from fixing games. It is not evidence of a huge match-fixing industry, although it is taken for granted that such a thing exists. In fact, by looking at the recent history of corruption in cricket, what becomes clear is not that the sport has an endemic problem with match-fixing, but that pulling off a successful fix is extraordinarily difficult. This is not to play down the danger that corruption poses to cricket; the number of attempts that have been made to throw matches in recent years is testament to that. But the Test match can only be protected if the nature of the threat is properly understood and too little has been written about what is required for a fix to work.

There are several reasons why successful examples of fixed Test

matches are hard to find. The most obvious is that the corrupt par-
ties have an interest in keeping the fix quiet. There are also softer
targets within the cricket calendar than a high-profile, televised
five-day game. But what the work of investigative journalists and
official commissions into corruption has shown is that match-fixing
is not as simple as it is frequently portrayed. As I was told by Stefan
Szymanski, an academic who has researched corruption in sport
extensively, "People think you lay down a lot of money, get the
outcome that you want and you walk away with a huge profit". In
fact, it is a complicated and sophisticated business, and its overall
success is reliant upon a group of disparate individuals each playing
their part correctly. The attempted fixes that have been uncovered
have been fragile, precarious ventures that have rarely gone to plan.
However, as Szymanski explained, "If the profit is large, then people
have the incentive to be sophisticated." And it is this idea—that
contemporary cricket provides too many incentives to potential
fixers—that should be of concern to the authorities.

These incentives are nothing new. Huge broadcasting deals and the
involvement of India's super-wealthy in the Indian Premier League
(IPL) mean that cricket has never been richer, but the sport has been
a plaything of wealthy patrons and feckless gamblers since the House
of Hanover was on the throne. The attraction is the nature of the
game itself. It is often said that, if you were to devise a sport to bet
on, you couldn't do better than cricket. Not only can you gamble
on the important stuff—the result and its margin—but also the size
of each innings, the number of runs each player will score, how he
will get out and who will take the next wicket. And below that, you
can bet on utterly banal things like the winner of the toss and the
number of extras. The possibilities are endless, and so the game has
been entertaining gamblers for more than 300 years.

In his seminal work, *A Social History of English Cricket*, Derek
Birley identified rising prosperity in 18th-century England as one
reason why gambling had become a "national addiction". Many had
disposable incomes for the first time, meaning that loose change was
burning holes in pockets. It was also a time of relaxing social mores,
which encouraged spending on entertainment. Among the elite, the
fashionable sport on which to bet was horse-racing, but cricket was
coming up fast on the inside. Birley identifies the blossoming of the

enthusiasm of the young Prince of Wales, Frederick Louis, as a key moment. His desire to be English was so strong that he had cricket bats shipped over to Hanover, where he was educated. When the prince moved to England, reports emerged of games played between members of the aristocracy where the prize money was a small fortune and the crowd comprised "many thousands of spectators of whom a great number were persons of distinction".

However, cricketers in the eighteenth century were not socially homogenous in the way that, for example, polo is today. The desire to make a living wherever possible meant that any occasion where money flowed freely attracted both high and low. Former British prime minister and amateur cricket historian, John Major, notes that, "A rough and tumble, or an illegal affray, was a frequent accompaniment to a competitive game or an unsettled bet, and in a violent age that may have been an added attraction." For the work-ing classes, the other popular sports of the age were bare-knuckle boxing and cock-fighting. Cricket was a less visceral attraction, but was also still to undergo its puritan Victorian makeover.

If cricket's sporting appeal transcended class, then so did the desire to bet on it. Among the patrons of the aristocracy, such as Sir William Gage or Edwin Stead, forming a team meant the opportunity to bet on its success, and wagers of 1,000 guineas were not unheard of. But, as the popularity of matches in London grew, bookmakers appeared on the periphery to cater for the gambling habit of the common man. One of cricket's early chroniclers, James Pycroft, recalls how, "Lord's was frequented by men with book and pencil, betting as openly and professionally as in the ring at Epsom, and ready to deal in the odds with any and every person of speculative propensities". So intertwined were cricket and betting that it is believed that the laying down of the first laws of the game at the Star and Garter pub in London in 1744 was done not to make matches comparable or to make it easier for the crowds to follow, but to resolve gambling disputes. The laws should be read in this context, and as such are less a parade of virtues than "a detailed catalogue of deviations from the path of righteous-ness", according to Birley. Likewise, many historians believe that averages were first published as a form guide. It is no exaggeration to say that players and patrons have been stretching the limits of fair play for longer than we have understood what playing fairly means.

It was inevitable that, once the laws had been established, they would be broken, and that gambling would be the motivation. Games were increasingly fixed by the start of the nineteenth century, occasionally with both sides attempting to lose. Billy Beldham, one of the pre-eminent players of the age, confessed to Pycroft that he and two of his teammates had agreed to lose a game for a team under the patronage of a Yorkshire landowner, George Osbaldeston, against a side representing Nottingham. The game had two twists: Pycroft discovered that the Nottingham team were also being paid to lose, and that playing for them was the Yorkshireman's arch-rival, Frederick Beauclerk. Such was the animosity between the two men that Beauclerk tried to counter his teammates' attempted sabotage, breaking a finger in blocking a deliberate overthrow. Beauclerk got his own back by having Osbaldeston's star player, William Lambert, banned from Lord's after he overheard Lambert discussing a fix in 1817.

The ostracising of Lambert seems to have been something of a turning point. The Marylebone Cricket Club (MCC) responded to cricket's first match-fixing scandal by banning bookmakers from Lord's and other grounds. This rather overlooked the fact—demonstrable in subsequent fixing scandals 150 years later—that rampant corruption undermines bookies too, as nobody, rich or poor, wants to bet on a match that they suspect might be fixed. Nor, of course, would people choose to watch a game where the outcome has already been decided. It may have been cricket's growing attraction as a spectator sport that prompted the MCC to make Lambert a scapegoat. Either way, its hard-line approach was one of the factors behind cricket's transformation in the nineteenth century.

The MCC was aided by a wave of social and technological developments that pushed cricket into the mainstream and made gambling (and match-fixing) less desirable. Foremost among these was the development of a widespread transport network. More roads, new canals, the first commercial railways and buses in cities combined to trigger a nationwide reconsideration of the concept of distance, and with it, the feasibility of travelling further for matches, both for players and spectators. The British press expanded, with the launch of *The Guardian*, *The Sunday Times*, *Bell's Life* and the *Daily News* in the first half of the nineteenth century, and reports on cricket matches fed the demand for copy. Finally, Pycroft and his peers buffed up cricket's reputation, reimagining it as symbolic of Victorian values. Thomas Hughes put it at the centre of *Tom Brown's School Days*, in which the eponymous hero discovered that "Football and cricket, now one comes to think of it, are such much better games than fives or hare-and-hounds, or any others where the object is to come in first or to win for oneself, and not that one's side may win." Unlike bare-knuckle boxing and cockfighting, which soon fell from favour, cricket was an ideal game for the Victorian sensibility, composed as it is of hours of honest toil in pursuit of collective, rather than individual, glory.

Where money was gambled on cricket in the Victorian age, it tended to be on business ventures that were designed to tap into the sport's growing popularity. One of the most successful bets was laid by William Clarke, who married the widowed landlady of a pub in Nottingham in 1838. At quite what stage in their courtship he noticed the empty plot of land behind the pub has gone unrecorded, but, within three years, he had roped it off and staged the first matches at his new Trent Bridge ground. This, however, was not Clarke's major innovation. His masterstroke was to spend £200 to tempt one of the country's leading batsmen, Fuller Pilch, to put together a team to play under the banner of 'England' at his ground. The event was such a success that Clarke then assembled a squad of the best professional players he could find to tour the country as the All-England Eleven, a cricketing precursor to the Harlem Globetrotters.[1]

Not even a natural entrepreneur such as Clarke could have predicted that the All-England Eleven would be such a runaway success. Its annual fixture list expanded to over 30 matches by 1851, helping to popularise the game throughout the country, especially in the north. The team's reputation was built on its performances on the field; Clarke carefully cultivated this image, according to Major, by inviting inferior sides to field up to 22 players against his 11. As his side continued to win, the legend grew that the All-England Eleven were literally twice as good as anyone else.

---

1   *Clarke's men were not cricketers by profession—in the mid-nineteenth century, there was no such thing—but men who had a trade, such as agricultural work or textile production, as opposed to being gentlemen.*

And as the fame of players such as Pilch, George Parr and Clarke himself spread across the land, so did the impresario's ability to charge higher appearance fees. The team's hosts were usually more than happy to spend the £70 required to bring Clarke's men to town (that, and a generous share of the gate receipts), because the match generated enough local interest for them to turn a profit. All of the team's income was channelled through Clarke, whose focus on the finances was as hawk-eyed as his field placings. His insistence on taking plenty off the top for himself was one of the reasons why, along with his expansion of the squad, he was the victim of a player rebellion in 1852, when John Wisden and Jemmy Dean established a rival side, the United All-England Eleven. Tired of seeing the bounty of a team effort going to just one man, Wisden built a side of equal quality, although it is not known whether the spoils were distributed more equitably. The two touring sides co-existed for several years, although it was only after Clarke's death in 1856 that they were allowed to play against each other. Three years after that, they were united in a combined England team that toured the United States.

It was not until the 1970s that the ban on bookies at cricket grounds was lifted. This was partly because cricket's Victorian reimagining meant that new corruption allegations risked staining it indelibly and partly because rumours of fixed matches never quite went away. Nevertheless, the return of the bookies seemed to have no ill effects on the game, although the players themselves were known to dabble. The Australian fast bowler, Dennis Lillee, in particular, was no stranger to a mid-game flutter. During the 1972 Ashes, he found himself carrying the drinks as 12th man when an Australian XI played a county match. To alleviate the boredom, he bet his teammates' cash on Australia taking five wickets before lunch. After they took six, he strolled over to collect his winnings and was furious to discover he had bet on five wickets and no more. Years later, he famously made up his losses and more by putting £10 on England winning the Headingley Test of 1981, at odds of 500-1. Lillee's actions attracted a front-page headline in *The Sun* ("Mystery of Aussie Bets Coup"), but no official censure. It was generally considered a bit of a laugh. Today, if an international player were discovered betting on his side to lose a match, his career would be over. The change in attitude is the result of the deathly procession of skeletons that walked out of cricket's closet at the turn of the millennium.

In April 2000 a Delhi police detective, Ishwar Singh Redhu, was going about his regular police work, investigating complaints of extortion made by several local businessmen. While listening in to a tapped phone, he stumbled on references to Hansie Cronje and then a conversation between the South Africa captain and an Indian man, Sanjay Chawla, in which the two discussed team selection and payments to players. When the story broke on April 7th, Cronje issued a statement passionately denying any wrongdoing. The cricket world generally believed him. He was a stoic, conservative and occasionally unimaginative player and captain; he would not have been at the top of anybody's list of corruptible players. He received strident support from his national board and coach as he tried to keep his head above water, one suspects in the hope that the Indian police were overstating the strength of their case. However, in Durban in the early hours of April 11th, he called Rory Steyn, one of the team's security managers, to his hotel room and admitted that there was truth to some of what had been reported in the media. It was the first of several partial confessions that he made when it became apparent that he was sinking fast.

Inevitably, questions began to be asked about whether Cronje was a one-off, or whether he was the proverbial bad apple that had rotted the entire sack. The cricket world stood nervously, shifting its weight from one foot to the other and wondering what was to come. Soon after Cronje made the headlines, the results of an enquiry led by a Pakistani judge, Malik Muhammad Qayyum, into the conduct of his country's national team were forced into the open. The investigation took place between August 1998 and October 1999, but the report had sat unopened (perhaps deliberately) on a government desk. A number of smaller-scale investigations into the team had been held over the past decade, but they had provided neither credible exonerations nor any convincing evidence. Qayyum's enquiry, however, had the heft of being commissioned by the federal government.

Qayyum recommended that a former Pakistani Test captain, Salim Malik, receive a life ban for attempting to fix a Test match against

Australia in 1994. During the course of the enquiry, Qayyum heard testimony from Shane Warne, which was supported independently by fellow Australian bowler, Tim May, that Malik had offered the pair US$200,000 to bowl badly and allow Pakistan to win. This was one of five incidents involving Malik that Qayyum investigated; in the other four cases, Qayyum found insufficient proof of the batsman's guilt.

Malik was one of eight cricketers whose actions were examined. Ata-ur-Rehman was also given a life ban, not for his involvement in corruption, but for perjuring himself while giving evidence against Wasim Akram. As for Wasim himself, Qayyum expressed his disappointment at his failure to co-operate with the investigation, and, given the number of unsubstantiated rumours surrounding the then captain, admitted, "He cannot be said to be above suspicion." Qayyum also recommended that he be stripped of the captaincy. Wasim's fellow opening bowler, Waqar Younis, was also censured for his "reluctance" to help the commission, for which Qayyum suggested that he be fined. Three more players, Inzamam-ul-Haq, Akram Raza and Saeed Anwar were also fined and criticised for their "partial amnesia" regarding the matches under investigation, with Qayyum convinced that they knew more than they were letting on.

As the Qayyum Report was digested in South Asia, an investigation in South Africa, supervised by a retired judge, Edwin King, heard the full extent of Cronje's involvement with bookmakers. In December 1996 Cronje was introduced to Mukesh "MK" Gupta, a bank clerk turned match-fixer, by the then Indian captain, Mohammad Azharuddin. Gupta, who was on the hunt for reliable sources to "forecast" matches—in effect, to provide inside information on team selection and the state of the pitch—gave Cronje US$30,000 (US$18,750) as a sweetener. This inducement sat around in Cronje's kitbag as it was transferred out of India, into and out of South Africa and then into England, committing several foreign-exchange violations in the process. Having seen Cronje take the bait, Gupta moved quickly. Days later, he offered Cronje the chance to throw a benefit game between India and South Africa for a former India player, Mohinder Amarnath, in exchange for US$200,000 (£125,000).

According to the testimonies given at the King Commission, morale in the South African team was low at this point. The team was at the end of a long tour around India, and many players were disgruntled that the Amarnath match had been upgraded in status to an official one-day international (ODI). Cronje approached a number of players privately as the team travelled to the game in Mumbai, before putting the offer in front of the entire team at a meeting. Former South Africa offspinner, Pat Symcox, described how several players refused, at which point Cronje said that the fix would only work if the whole team were committed to it. After that, according to Symcox, a small group of players, including himself, Brian McMillan, Dave Richardson and Cronje were joking about it and decided to see how far Gupta would go. Cronje phoned him and managed to get the price pushed up by US$50,000. But Cronje again refused the fix, as he lacked the support of the whole team.

Despite this disappointment, Gupta continued to ply Cronje with funds in exchange for information. Cronje was given another US$50,000 on January 10th 1997, and, in return, he told Gupta when he would declare during a Test match against India. (Neither declaration made by Cronje in the match concerned was unusual in the context of the game, unlike the England game in 2000.) Finally, a third tranche, of US$30,000, was paid five days later; Cronje told the Commission that he thought Gupta was "more than happy" with the information provided in exchange, something that Gupta later denied. After a further attempt to approach Cronje a few months later was rebuffed, the relationship ended.

It is either heavily ironic or a reflection of how close the relationship between cricket and gamblers had become that Cronje was approached by a second fixer, Marlon Aronstam, three years later. There is no evidence of a relationship between Gupta and Aronstam, and there was no suggestion that Aronstam approached Cronje because he knew him to be corrupt. According to Aronstam's testimony, he sought out Cronje solely because he was the South Africa captain, and therefore had the ability to determine the course of the match. He had no idea that he was rekindling an urge that, as Cronje confessed to the King Commission, was akin to drug or alcohol addiction.

After Centurion, Cronje was approached again, this time by one of several men who clung to the coat-tails of the South Africa team, a biltong seller called Hamid Cassim. He in turn introduced Cronje to Sanjay Chawla, whom Cronje believed to be a punter. At a

hotel in Durban, Chawla and Cassim asked Cronje to provide them
with information during South Africa's forthcoming tour to India and
suggested that he could earn a lot of money if he were prepared to
fix a game. Cronje gave them sufficient encouragement—suggesting
that he would be prepared to fix a dead rubber—such that he left the
room with around US$15,000 hidden in a mobile-phone box. At the
Commission, Cronje described how Chawla grew more aggressive and
persistent during the tour to India. His interest in information about
the pitch waned. What he really wanted was Cronje to persuade his
colleagues to underperform. Cronje attempted to bluff his way out.
He said that he had the players on side, but that they had failed to
fix a one-day game in the way that he had planned. It appears that
Chawla saw through this rather lame ploy, and he continued to lean
on Cronje. In response, during the Test series Cronje told first Pieter
Strydom, and then Jacques Kallis, Mark Boucher and Lance Klusener,
in a "semi-serious" manner that there was a man willing to pay them
to play badly. Each of the players turned him down.

Ahead of the fifth ODI in Nagpur, Cronje received another call from
Chawla, insisting that he fix the game. This time, Cronje approached
other teammates: batsman, Herschelle Gibbs, and bowler, Henry
Williams. Gibbs was to receive US$15,000 for scoring fewer than 20;
Williams was bribed with a similar amount to concede more than
50. Cronje told Chawla that the cost of bringing both players into
the fix would be US$50,000, suggesting that he was sufficiently calm
about the process to ensure a hefty fee for himself. The plan was for
South Africa to score no more than 270 runs. Evidently, Gibbs did
not take Cronje seriously—he scored 74 at more than a run a ball
as South Africa racked up 320. Williams also failed to hold up his
end of the bargain, as he was injured while bowling his second over.
According to Cronje, Cassim approached the captain on Chawla's
behalf, again ahead of a one-day tournament in March 2000, but
he declined to speak to him. A month later, the Indian police went
public with their discoveries.

The final set of revelations came in November 2000, when Delhi's
Central Bureau of Investigation (CBI) released the findings of the
investigation it had launched after accidentally listening in on Cronje.
Like Qayyum, the CBI was dismayed by the "conspiracy of silence"
maintained by the "cricket fraternity", which impeded its progress.

It did, however, manage to extract a testimony from MK Gupta that added in several missing pieces to the Cronje jigsaw.

Gupta had spent the majority of the 1980s learning about cricket, following a hunch that there was money to be made as an illegal bookmaker. His knowledge soon paid dividends and he progressed up the chain of bookies in Delhi, handling bigger and bigger bets. He describes how he spotted a talented young cricketer, Ajay Sharma, in a club game in 1988 and gave him Rp2,000 (£22) "as a token of his appreciation" and told him to keep in touch. Gupta's backing of Sharma proved a shrewd investment: he was soon playing for the India one-day team and relaying information on pitches, weather and team selection back to Gupta. In his statement to the CBI, Sharma denied this involvement, but admitted introducing Gupta to a team-mate, Manoj Prabhakar.

Gupta courted Prabhakar in the same way in which he had courted Sharma, as he sought to move further and further up the cricket hierarchy in search of the men who were influential enough to illicitly influence the outcome of a match. Through Prabhakar, he met other notable players: New Zealand's Martin Crowe; Sri Lanka's Aravinda de Silva and Arjuna Ranatunga; Pakistan's Salim Malik; Brian Lara of the West Indies; and Australia's Dean Jones and Mark Waugh. Money was often paid to Prabhakar to make these introductions.

As one would hope, most of these meetings were ultimately fruitless. Gupta claimed to have paid US$20,000 and US$40,000 to Crowe and Jones, respectively, for information, but neither provided anything of substance and refused to become more involved. Malik proved a fickle ally: Gupta recalled paying the Pakistani Rs800,000 (around £9,000) to fix a game between domestic cup winners in India and Pakistan in the early 1990s, and also making money on Malik's information on a Singer Cup game between Australia and Pakistan in 1996. But, on other occasions, Malik backed away from him. Gupta made strong allegations that the two Sri Lankans underperformed to fix a Test against India in Lucknow in 1994, which the home team duly won by an innings and 119 runs. Gupta claims that he gave de Silva US$15,000 after the end of the match. Between them, de Silva and Ranatunga made 33 runs in four innings, although Sri Lanka's overall performance was so abject that it is hard to see that Gupta's alleged investment was money well spent. An investigation was launched by the Sri Lanka Cricket Board (SLCB, now Sri Lanka Cricket) into Gupta's claims. The two were exonerated by one of Sri Lanka's most prominent lawyers, Desmond Fernando, largely because he was unable to persuade Gupta to support his accusations.

The most important relationship cultivated by Gupta was that with the then Indian captain, Mohammad Azharuddin. Neither man is clear on how they met. Gupta told the CBI that Prabhakar introduced them during a Sri Lankan tour to India (which would suggest it was some time in 1994); Azharuddin remembered the intermediary being Ajay Sharma, and that the first meeting was in New Delhi in 1995. Regardless, this must have felt to Gupta like his big break. For a fixer, Azharuddin was India's most influential player, and was willing not just to give information, but to "do" matches. However, the skipper was to prove a disappointing and unreliable accomplice.

Azharuddin agreed to fix games at an international one-day triangular tournament, the Titan Cup between South Africa, India and Australia in 1996. The details of the fix have not been made public, but, according to Gupta, he lost a lot of money on the matches, which India won by 35 runs. Azharuddin subsequently gave accurate information to Gupta about two of India's Test matches against South Africa later in the same year, which helped to reduce Gupta's losses. Neither man suggested that these games were fixed. Gupta continued to persevere with Azharuddin, often receiving information via Azharuddin's wife, Sangeeta Bijlani, but many of these tips turned out to be incorrect, to the extent that Gupta worried that the pair were also involved with other bookies. It was for this reason that Gupta leveraged Azharuddin's contacts to secure an introduction to another Test captain: Hansie Cronje.

Gupta told the CBI that he had given up all involvement in India's illegal betting industry in May 1998. One particular series may have convinced him that enough was enough. Having met Cronje and filled the player's infamous kitbag with US$30,000 in late 1996, the South African then gave Gupta assurances that his team would lose several matches in a forthcoming ODI series with India. However, South Africa beat India comfortably in all four matches. Gupta says that Cronje apologised afterwards, suggesting that India had played so badly that he had no hope of manipulating the game so that South Africa would lose. Gupta must have watched the series in despair. He had paid handsome incentives to the captain of one side and a former captain of the other, but neither was able to deliver the results that he had been told to expect. Gupta discovered that, even when all of the pieces are in place, a fix can still prove elusive.

After the contents of the Qayyum and CBI reports were made public, and the King Commission had handed down a life ban to Cronje, the ICC juddered into action. In mid-2000 it hired a former Metropolitan Police Commissioner, Sir Paul Condon, to run an anti-corruption unit (ACSU), to back up national cricket boards and police in their investigations. The ease with which Gupta, in particular, was able to ingratiate himself with Test players from every nation showed that fixing had become a global concern, beyond the jurisdiction of any single national-level investigation. In a 2001 report, Condon described much the same situation as Qayyum, a "conspiracy of silence" that led him to believe that the "allegations in the public domain were only the tip of the iceberg". However, unlike Qayyum, who was inclined to believe that it was the players' complicity in corruption that prevented them from co-operating, Condon blamed the lack of a system to "receive or process reports of improper approaches or behaviour". In other words, without a way to blow the whistle confidentially, players were worried about being exposed as a grass.

The ACSU responded by setting up a private phone line and email address for players to report illegal approaches; unsurprisingly, there is no data available to indicate how frequently they have been used. The ACSU also requires all international players to follow a strict code of conduct; an unambiguous document that would seem to outlaw all potentially corrupt activities, and which, should it be required, can demand access to phone and bank records. In no other sport is player behaviour governed by so onerous a code. Mobile phones were banned from the dressing rooms of international teams, and security tightened around the players during international matches. Condon has also spoken of a database compiled by intelligence managers that "adheres to all the high standards of data protection. All manner of people input details: police forces, intelligence services, our own staff. Bookmakers, legitimate and unlawful, would be on there because we have memoranda of understanding with people like Betfair [the online betting exchange]. Also, we have informants among the unlawful bookmakers, primarily in India." This database is, then, used to compile blacklists of suspected troublemakers to be banned from ICC events.

Finally, through its regional security managers, the ACSU has established a presence at most international matches. The role of the security manager is somewhere between a spy and a Samaritan. They are available as the first contact for players and support staff to report illegal approaches or suspicious behaviour and to remind them of their responsibilities under the anti-corruption code. But they are also on the look-out for known fixers and punters and new information to add to the database. The difficulty is that the number of countries playing international cricket is larger than the number of managers, which means each is assigned to two teams. The problem, as Ed Hawkins has identified, is that the two teams for which a manager is responsible are often playing matches at the same time on different continents. How can a manager ensure that players can talk to him at the drop of a hat when he is only intermittently available? The hiring of five more part-time managers was among 27 recommendations made to the International Cricket Council (ICC) about the operation of the ACSU by an independent review in 2011. So far, two have been appointed. Providing an always-available contact on the off chance that a player has information to pass on is a huge drain on limited resources (remember that Cronje's initial confession to Rory Steyn took place in the middle of the night in the team hotel) and means that it is a pretty inefficient operation. But to withdraw the managers would look like the ICC's commitment to its own anti-corruption campaign were wavering.

Despite the measures it has taken in the past decade, the ACSU has frequently been criticised. A trio of England captains have spoken out against it: Andrew Strauss described it as "a toothless tiger"; Geoffrey Boycott claimed it was mere "window dressing"; and Michael Vaughan asked simply, "What does it do?" This exaspera-tion is partly because of a lack of demonstrable results: only two cricketers, Marlon Samuels of the West Indies and Maurice Odumbe of Kenya, have been banned as a result of the ACSU's investigations (and the unit was tipped off on Samuels by the Indian police). Yet to suggest that the ACSU is failing because it has suspended "only" two players is to presuppose that a much bigger number have been engaged in corruption. The Unit is therefore in a difficult position. If it were working perfectly, it would be handing down no suspensions at all, as it would have deterred all cricketers from corruption. As it is, the ACSU needs players to break the rules to justify its existence, but the more this occurs, the weaker it appears.

It is also fair to suggest that the ACSU's role has frequently been misunderstood. When corruption has been exposed by anyone other than the ACSU, it is the Unit that has been blamed for missing it. But the Unit is not the cricket police. It has no judicial or law-enforcing powers. As Condon's successor, Sir Ronnie Flanagan, argued: "We cannot arrest, we cannot engage in the sorts of undercover operations of which the police engage. The only power we have is the power vested in us by the ICC." Nor does it have the budget to conduct lengthy and expensive observations of suspected fixers or corrupt players. The limits of its circumstances mean that it is suited only to player education and security.

There are two areas, however, where the ACSU has underperformed. One is in recruiting staff with sufficient knowledge of cricket. Vaughan wrote in *The Daily Telegraph* in 2011, "It is a fact that the AC[S]U is run by former police officers who have personally told me in the past they do not fully understand the game. They know about corruption and how to gather telephone evidence and emails, but do not have a clue about spotting when something untoward happens on a cricket pitch." Vaughan's comments are given credence by the embarrassing moment in the Pakistan spot-fixing trial when the ACSU's former chief investigator, Ravi Sawani, professed that he did not know what a bracket was. Scyld Berry said there was "overt amazement" in the courtroom during his giving evidence. If Sawani's ignorance is representative of the Unit as a whole, then it is difficult to see how it can succeed in identifying corruption even while it is unfolding in front of its eyes.

The second area is a failure to fully investigate the tip-offs that it receives. Evidence given at the spot-fixing trial revealed that the

ACSU was passed information from a source, believed to be an ex-member of Pakistan's support staff, that members of the team were involved in throwing matches during the team's tour to Australia in 2009/10 and again at the World Twenty20 (T20) in the West Indies. The ACSU is believed to have received an initial tip-off, and then, several months later, copies of text messages to members of the Pakistan team downloaded from the phone of a suspected fixer, Mazhar Majeed. According to Nick Hoult of *The Telegraph*, the source only went to the *News of the World* newspaper when the ACSU showed no sign of progressing in its investigation. By August 2010 the paper had set up a sting operation and three corrupt Pakistani players had been exposed.

It is not strictly fair to compare the ACSU and the *News of the World*, as the playing field is uneven. The ACSU is governed by strict entrapment laws in the UK, which rightly prevent employees from offering inducements to tempt their workers. For the newspaper, there are no such restrictions; the sting was a piece of investigative journalism *par excellence*. The trial also revealed that the paper was still missing US$100,000 of the payments that it made to Majeed. It could swallow this, given the publicity the story created and the extra copies that were sold. But one assumes that a similar sum would blow a giant hole in the ACSU's budget. Nevertheless, it feels like an institutional failure that a member of the Pakistani inner circle was obliged to seek out an investigative journalist to expose corruption because the sport's anti-corruption body failed, or was unable, to act on his information.

In fact, the ACSU wasted the best chance that we have had since Centurion to understand how match-fixing works, because the *News of the World* sting, for all of its shock value, actually told us very little about what sort of a threat Test cricket faces from corruption. There is art to the investigations that its reporter, Mazher Mahmood, has built a career out of, but he is a generalist, he is not an expert in cricket or illegal gambling. The sum of what we learned about corruption from the so-called spot-fixing scandal was that there were several players in the Pakistan team who were vulnerable to offers of cash for some low-level cheating. That was all. No bets were laid, despite Majeed apparently having Salman Butt, Mohammad Asif and Mohammad Amir in his pocket. The *News of the World* had no interest in exploring the other half of the fix: that is, how money is made. Exposing the Pakistanis was enough. Had the ACSU been quicker off the mark, it is possible that the lid could have been lifted on a world that remains almost entirely out of reach. Even worse than this, the scandal also perpetrated several inaccuracies about match-fixing that have yet to be properly scrutinised. However, when considered correctly, they help to explain why successful fixing is so rare in Test cricket.

First, we need to be clear about what actually went on at Lord's in August 2010. To everybody in the ground, myself included, the answer at the time was a great Test match. England were 39-1 after the first day was all but completely washed out by rain. At the start of the second day, 18 year-old Mohammad Amir took the wickets of Alastair Cook, Kevin Pietersen, Paul Collingwood and Eoin Morgan without conceding a run, to leave the home side in desperate trouble at 47-5. He then added the scalps of Matt Prior and Graeme Swann later in the innings. At the other end, his partner, Mohammad Asif, was scarcely less impressive, demonstrating such control that England could barely score a run against him, despite his bowling at little over 70mph. I was riveted, as was everyone around me. It's a testament to the cricketing excellence of these two men that they were able to wreak such havoc at the same time as being involved in a conspiracy.

The previous day, Amir had overstepped by nine inches on the third ball of the third over, and Asif—a much calmer character—bowled a fractional no-ball with the sixth ball of the tenth. On the second day, Amir delivered an even bigger no-ball, missing the line of the crease by a foot, with the third ball of his third full over. It is commonly assumed that Amir bowled such obvious no balls because he was young, nervous and eager to please. However, in a conversation between Majeed and Mahmood at a London hotel on the day before the Test, the fixer told the journalist, "They will be well over the line" because "we're not paying the umpire". Amir followed the script to the letter, not wishing to run the risk of the umpire failing to notice the no-ball, and consequently his signal to Mahmood. In exchange for arranging the no-balls, Majeed received two payments, the first of £10,000 and the second of £140,000. The sting was complete when £1,500 worth of the marked bills given to Majeed by Mahmood were later found in Amir's hotel room and £2,500 of the newspaper's money was recovered from the room of Salman Butt.

Signalling was what this was about. The men were cheating, of that there is no doubt, because, as Brian Phillips has pithily explained, "The essential idea of athletic competition—let's both show up and try to win—[was] no longer operating". But Lord's 2010 was not the same as Centurion 2000, and not only because it was single deliveries rather than the outcome of the match that were being tampered with. Unlike Centurion, there was no Marlon Aronstam on the other end. There was no-one attempting to cash in on Majeed's control over the players. This was a very under-reported part of the story. As Stefan Syzmanski suggests, people assume that, if you spend the money to buy the players, the profits generate themselves.

But it is not as simple as that. Suppose that, instead of the *News of the World*, which was interested only in exposing the players, Majeed had been approached by a genuine punter, who was out to profit from the fix. For the sake of argument, we'll call him Azhar. Azhar would have to approach an illegal bookmaker to avoid leaving a paper trail that could expose the scam if the players were caught or confessed. It is frequently assumed that Azhar would speak to an illegal bookmaker in India and ask for odds on Amir bowling a no-ball with the third ball of his third full over on the second day. But if you were the bookmaker, what odds would you give him? 5-1? 10-1? Or would the specificity of his bet not ring alarm bells? Why would you possibly seek out a bookmaker for such a precise bet unless you had inside information? Azhar would have no more luck laying this bet in India that he would with the licensed bookies in Lord's itself. Betting in India may be illegal and outside of the tax net, but the principles that bookmakers operate under are the same.

There are other strategies that Azhar could use to disguise the fix. He could water down his bet, to whether Amir would bowl any no balls in the over, but he would be offered meaner odds. He could also reduce the size of the stake and spread it across a number of different bookmakers, in the hope of appearing like a regular, uninformed punter. Ed Hawkins, who has thought along similar lines, got his calculator out, and, on the basis that Azhar would be dealing with small-time bookmakers who accepted wagers of no more than Rs25,000 (around £300) at a time, discovered that, if he were able to get odds of even money, he would need to lay 490 bets in order to match the £150,000 that he had to pay Majeed to arrange the fix. Furthermore, it is unlikely that he would be able to repeat the trick with the same bookmakers in the future, as they would soon smell a rat. At such a rate, his fixing career would be over before it had begun. Given that fixing is cheating, and supposed to be an easier way to get ahead than working honestly, such a process seems like awfully hard work.

Instead, the no-balls were nothing more than Majeed making his capabilities clear, a message to the newspaper (or, rather, the syndicate that Mahmood claimed to represent). *I have them under control. Now let's make some money.* But how could a punter such as Azhar capitalise on Majeed's influence over Butt, Asif and Amir?

One of the great unknowns in the cricket world is which markets are available to bet on in India. It is the crucial missing piece of the jigsaw. Over the course of my research, I received several different answers from credible sources. Where there was agreement, however, is on the fact that the number of markets is very limited, which has crucial implications for how matches are fixed. It is the belief of everyone with whom I spoke that the most obvious and straightforward market to bet on is the winner of the match. Gamblers can back this in forward markets ahead of the game, or live, as the match progresses. The second is the number of runs scored in an innings. This, again, can be bet on before or during the game. Bookies typically offer a range of runs, such as 305-325, and gamblers can bet that the total will be above or below it. I was told that it is possible to put spread bets on this, which would enable much larger profits and losses.[2]

---

2   *Suppose that a punter thought the batting team would score fewer than 305 runs. If he bet below the spread at Rp100 a run and the team scored 250, he would make Rs5,500 profit. But, if the team went on to make 420, he would owe the bookie Rp11,500.*

The third market commonly believed to be on offer is the one that foxed Ravi Sawani: brackets. I have heard that brackets can be as short as five overs (known sometimes in India as *choti paari*) or as long as ten overs (*lambi paari*). Brackets are only available once the match has begun and refer to the number of runs scored in a fixed number of overs. Like the previous market, it involves a spread bet on the number of runs being above or below an offered range. I was told by several sources that bookmakers would not accept serious money on "fancy bets" (betting on tiny elements of the game, such as the number of no-balls or the number of players wearing sunglasses).

There is logic behind Indian bookmakers' offering only a very limited number of markets. If the bookmaker accepted bets on any aspect of the game, he would be certain to end up paying out on bets that were fixed. Given the volume of bets that are laid during a game, bookies do not have the time to consider the cleanliness of each bet. It makes far more sense to take as many bets as possible on a small number of markets that punters cannot easily manipulate.

It also follows that bookies have an incentive to keep their markets clean, as punters would be reluctant to bet with a bookmaker that was known to be involved in fixing. However, reports have emerged in recent years, including that by Hawkins, which suggest that the illegal bookmaking industry is very stratified, with bookies working under a chief or kingpin, who determines the odds and passes them down to his workers. Under this system, where bookies do not know which, if any, elements of matches are fixed, their incentive to maintain a clean industry disappears. The most important thing to them is maintaining their place in the syndicate by encouraging their punters to gamble.

But let us return to the markets and see how a match might be fixed in such a way that could allow Azhar to make money on the outcome. Suppose that, instead of bribing Amir and Asif, Azhar and Majeed had bribed the two opening batsmen, and that they had arranged to both get out in consecutive overs, say the 21st and the 22nd of the innings. As it is not possible to bet on when a batsman will get out, according to Hawkins, the best bet that Azhar could lay would be on the number of runs scored in a bracket. Azhar would look for the bookie offering the highest spread of runs to be scored in a bracket covering the 21st over to the 30th, and then bet that the batting team would score fewer than that. The logic behind this is that batsmen, particularly in Test matches, like to take time to play themselves in, and so, after the two corrupt openers had fallen quickly, Azhar could be reasonably confident that the run-rate would slow. As the bookmaker would have no idea that the batsmen were certain to get out, his odds would reflect only the standard factors that bookies consider: the pitch, the weather, the quality of the bowlers and the reputations of the batsmen. Azhar should, in this case, be able to make a profit on his inside information.

However, from a fixer's perspective, there are several unsatisfactory risks about this fix, which mean that the money used to bribe the batsmen might not be well spent. The first is that the batsmen may inadvertently get themselves out before the designated overs. The risk of the corrupt players being unable to deliver what they have promised is a standard risk in any fix and might be acceptable to the fixer—provided that there aren't other large risks. But, in this case, there are. The incoming batsmen, numbers three and four, may decide that, in order to wrest the initiative back from the bowling side, they are going to take a chance and bat aggressively from the beginning, pushing up the run rate. Or the fielding captain might make a mistake and rotate his bowlers or change his field in such a way that suits the new batsmen and enables them to score quickly. It's also possible that the opening batsmen are only able to score slowly in the first 20 overs, which means that the spread is lower than the fixer would like. There are plenty of other potential risks, too.[3]

....

3 There may be an easier way to fix elements of matches, but it only really works in limited-overs games. In these matches, the spreads offered for the number of runs scored in a bracket are higher than in Tests because the run-rates are faster. So, suppose that Azhar had bribed one of the opening batsmen to play out a maiden over, as Salman Butt was intended to have done, at one stage, for Majeed. In a Test match, six dot balls within a bracket of ten overs would have little effect on the odds offered by a bookmaker, because typical run-rates in Test matches are low—between 2.5 and 3.5 runs an over. There might also be plenty of time for the batsmen to catch up to the expected rate in the remaining overs. But in an ODI or T20 game, the run rates are much higher—6 or 8 an over—which means that there is more room to bet under the spread and win. The risk is that there is a higher chance of the players' unusual behaviour being detected, as maidens are less common in limited-overs cricket. It is unclear whether this form of spot-fixing has ever been attempted. Five players were suspended from the IPL in 2012 after one was caught in a sting by a television channel negotiating to bowl no-balls, but, as in the Pakistan case, it does not appear that money was to be wagered on their behaviour.

Despite the risks of attempting to fix a Test through brackets, it would seem that they are actually the least problematic for fixers, which suggests how difficult it is to arrange fixes using the others. The total number of runs in an innings is almost impossible to fix without the co-operation of an entire team. Hansie Cronje attempted to keep South Africa's score under 270 runs in the Nagpur ODI in 2000 using only Herschelle Gibbs and Henry Williams, and Gibbs ignored him, scoring 74 at more than a run a ball. Bribing a whole team is expensive, as Cronje found when he made his offer to the team in Mumbai in 1996. Even when US$250,000 was on the table, some players still voted with their conscience.

It is also difficult to imagine a set of circumstances that would enable a single player, or even a small group of players, to exploit the other market—the outcome of the match. It is telling that the only fixed Test match we known of—Centurion in 2000—was manipulated on the fly. Aronstam's approach to Cronje was not premeditated. It was a piece of opportunism generated by the unusual weather.

A match that is frequently described as suspicious is the Sydney Test between Australia and Pakistan in January 2010. Majeed boasted to Mahmood that he made £1.3m from the game by betting on the match result. He claimed to have received odds of 40-1 on Australia winning the game when they had a lead of just 51 with just two wickets remaining in their second innings. They recovered to set Pakistan a total of 176, with the visitors collapsing to 139 all out. The circumstances are unusual, but they were hardly Headingley 1981. Moreover, it is difficult to see where any cheating occurred. Fingers have been pointed at the wicketkeeper, Kamran Akmal, who dropped four chances during the Australian second innings. But three of those drops were made before the point when Majeed claims to have put his bet on. Up to this point, Akmal would have had no incentive to mess up. It is possible to argue that he knew that a fix was planned and so he was worried that Australia would collapse and lose by an innings (thereby depriving Pakistan of a chance to capitulate). However, at the time he was dropping the ball, Australia were only four and five wickets down, so this seems unlikely.

Furthermore, in Pakistan's run chase, several of the batsmen were out to excellent catches; Salman Butt chose to refer an LBW decision and managed to get it overturned; and Mohammad Sami chose not to walk after nicking a catch behind, forcing Australia to refer it. Surely if they were trying to lose the match, the men would have walked?[4] In all likelihood, Pakistan lost through sheer ineptitude, yet most people still believe that the game was dubious. Given the media's predisposition to suspicion, the likelihood of being able to hide a fix that involves most of the team on something as closely scrutinised as the match result looks remote. So this market, too, poses problems for fixers.

The main point is that having a small number of markets means that the relationship between the behaviour that the corrupt player is being paid to exhibit (such as bowling a no-ball) and the element of the game that the fixer is gambling on (such as the match result) is less direct. And the less direct the relationship between the two elements of the fix, the smaller the chance of it succeeding. To the best of our knowledge, none of the available markets in India allows direct bets on behaviours that can be directly manipulated by fixers. This is the reason why the number of fixed Test matches is so small.

Stefan Szymanski has written that there are two difficulties when it comes to fixing: laying large enough bets to ensure a good profit, but without the sums being so large that they raise suspicion; and preventing the odds from shifting so that the return becomes negligible. Our knowledge about recent fixing in cricket enables us to add a third challenge: finding a market that is not so tangential to the corrupt players that their influence on the fix is insignificant.

The past decade and a half has not been the golden age for match-fixers that it is commonly assumed to have been. Fixers have been incentivised to encourage corruption in cricket by the huge increase in the money that has flowed into the sport through larger broadcasting and advertising deals and the rising wealth of India. But the exposés of corrupt players and the existence of the ACSU, for

---

4   For a fuller explanation of why it is unlikely the match was fixed, see Geoff Lemon's article in The Roar, entitled 'Was the Sydney Test rigged?'

all its flaws, has kept fixing in the spotlight. The greater attention paid to this form of cheating, together with the self-regulation of the Indian gambling industry, have ensured that the number of fixed Test matches has remained very small.

But what about the players themselves? Sir Paul Condon, in his 2001 report, identified several factors that he believed had allowed corruption to take root in the sport. Inevitably, given the ACSU's reach, these involved players, rather than fixers. The progress that has been made in neutralizing these factors has been decidedly mixed in the years since the report was published, which makes it difficult to argue, as Condon has done, that there has been a "seismic shift" in the relationship between players and match-fixing since the ACSU was established.

The first of Condon's factors—that international crickets are paid less than the players at the pinnacle of other sports—has been directly affected by the biggest change in cricket since 2001: the rise of the franchise. It is quite straightforward to see that underpaid elite sportsmen are particularly vulnerable to corruption, as not only are they likely to be talented and influential enough to be useful to a fixer, but the wage disparity with their contemporaries in other sports means that they have an incentive to boost their income illegally. In the mid-1990s top English or Australian Test cricketers typically earned in a year what Premier League footballers earned in a week. Despite the phenomenal growth in wages in football in the past 20 years, this wealth gap has actually shrunk, and it is all because of the IPL and its imitators.

For those able to attract a big IPL contact, it is now possible to earn many times more from six weeks of playing T20 than from playing international cricket for a year. It is true that the majority of international cricketers are better off, regardless of their participation in the T20 jamboree (because higher broadcasting revenue has led to wages rising faster than domestic inflation rates), but for those that have found employment in the IPL and elsewhere, the effect on income has been truly transformative. According to research by Sporting Intelligence, the average salary in the IPL in 2011 was US$486,228. Of course, this represents the six most lucrative weeks of the year for a cricketer, and their annual salary would have to be the same as their IPL earnings on a pro-rata basis to match those of a top footballer or an elite tennis player, but the highest-earning cricketers can at least now afford to eat at the same table as other leading sportspeople.

Importantly, the rise of franchise cricket has also offered players a totally different source of income. Previously, a player's sole income was that which he could earn from playing international cricket, supplemented with occasional appearances for his county or state. Players from cricket's poorer relations—the West Indies, Pakistan, Sri Lanka and Bangladesh—where the national boards pay badly, had no alternative sources of income, outside of corruption. The IPL changed all that. According to *Forbes* magazine's latest survey of the world's highest-paid athletes, MS Dhoni earned US$31.5m in the year to June 2013, making him 16th on the list. He earned more than Wayne Rooney, Novak Djokovic and Alex Rodriguez. No cricketer would have been earning enough to be mixing with Premier League footballers and Formula 1 drivers in the pre-IPL era, not even Sachin Tendulkar. As a result, it now seems inconceivable, from an economic perspective at least, that cricket's biggest stars could be tempted by money in brown envelopes from fixers because they felt the need to boost their income. They now earn so much from cricket that the bribes and incentives from fixing are just not powerful enough.

The IPL appears to have put Condon's primary concern to rest. However, it is too simplistic to say that T20 franchises have eliminated players' primary vulnerability to fixers. Not every professional cricketer can compete in the IPL, and not only because the IPL is a meritocracy. No Pakistani players have been chosen by a franchise since the attacks on Mumbai in November 2008. Was it, therefore, a coincidence that the first major corruption scandal to emerge since the launch of the IPL involved the excluded Pakistanis? Much has been made of the fact that Mohammad Amir was paid just £30,000 a year by the Pakistan Cricket Board (PCB), plus Test match fees. That might seem a small fortune in a country where the average income is one-tenth of that figure, but Amir spent his life among other international sportsmen. His rural upbringing in the Punjab had been left behind. And where underpaid West Indians or Bangladeshis would be auditioning for the IPL, that route was unavailable to Amir and Asif.

The worry, then, should not be that international cricketers are paid less than their counterparts in other sports, but that the rise of franchise cricket has seen the wage disparity between the most famous cricketers in the world and the regular county or state pros widen into a chasm. Gideon Haigh sees professional cricket as divided into "haves with a sense of entitlement" and "have-nots with a sense of grievance". Does this matter? In terms of corruption in Test matches, perhaps not, for two reasons. First, most Test players, are among the wealthier professional cricketers, as a result of being adequately paid for their skills by national boards and attracting sponsorships or a lucrative franchise contract every year. The threshold for a player to become tempted by corruption will vary between individuals, but income opportunities have been transformed, even in the short time since the Cronje scandal, which means that fewer ought to have their heads turned. Second, there is likely to be a positive correlation between the players that fixers need in their pockets and the players on higher incomes. Fixers need influential players, such as captains, opening batsmen and opening bowlers, in order to ensure that the game runs to a plan. And it is these high-profile cricketers that are likely to receive higher wages and sponsorships and so be less vulnerable to fixing.

If cricket's biggest stars are now out of the reach of fixers, it follows that there should be greater concern about those further down cricket's food chain, where salaries are smaller and oversight of games is patchier. It has become fashionable to suggest that state or county matches are the new frontier in fixing, particularly since ESPN Star Sports bought rights to show English county matches live on television in India in 2012. This deal coincided with the first conviction of an English player for corruption. Mervyn Westfield was found guilty of conspiracy to defraud after accepting a £6,000 bribe to bowl badly for Essex. Demonstrating once again how difficult it is to fix a match, Essex's opponents, Durham, were only able to score ten runs from the over, when Westfield was instructed to concede 12. The bowler certainly tried his best, delivering four wides and a no-ball.

The IPL has been dogged by rumours that players are involved in similar sorts of fixing. In 2012 five players were suspended, one of whom, TP Sudhindra, was banned for life for bowling a no-ball to order. But it is difficult to discern any sort of trend from these incidents or the Westfield case, particularly as the IPL players were stung by a TV station, India TV, in the same manner as Butt, Asif and Amir were implicated by the *News of the World*. Again, the avarice of players was exposed, but the cases did not produce any evidence that fixers were approaching players. Whether county or state cricket is attractive to match-fixers ultimately depends on the amount of money that is bet on the games. Large, fraudulent bets of the sort that interest fixers are more easily hidden among the huge sums that are bet on international matches. Such bets should be more conspicuous among the smaller totals wagered on minor games. It is fair to say that, to date, even if a greater disparity in wages is predisposing the sport's poorer relations to corruption, there is little evidence, yet, that fixers have found a way to exploit it.

Another of Condon's primary reasons for the spread of corruption was the lack of a structure in place for the authorities to receive information about potential fixing. This is an area where there has been undeniable progress, and it is no longer an excuse for players to fail to report their suspicions. Each national board now has its own anti-corruption code, in addition to that of the ICC, while players in major tournaments are required to attend briefings on how they might be approached. The most demonstrable measure of this progress was the Westfield case. For six months, his teammate, Tony Palladino, knew that Westfield had received money for his dodgy over, but did not know what he could do with his information. Then he attended a talk by the Professional Cricketers' Association (PCA) and realised that he could report what he knew. Nevertheless, Palladino's story is not a universally positive one: he received abuse from supporters and chose to move from Essex to Derbyshire to start again. There is still work to do to remove the stigma attached to blowing the whistle, but the progress made to provide support for players is undeniable.

The same cannot be said, however, about the third of Condon's factors: the number of meaningless matches. He identified one-day tournaments in neutral venues, such as Singapore or Sharjah in the late 1990s, as particularly vulnerable to corruption. Security was typically lax, allowing unsavoury characters to mix easily with players. These tournaments were also pretty casual affairs, meaning that players could underperform without feeling like they were putting their careers in jeopardy. Such tournaments have since fallen from favour, but their place in the fixture calendar has been taken by the countless T20 tournaments that seek to replicate the IPL.

In late 2011, Condon told *The Cricketer,* "The 'anything goes' party atmosphere [of T20 cricket] allowed some really bad people back into the game. Some of the notorious fixers from the early years started to re-emerge on the circuit in India, Pakistan, South Africa, Australia and the UK… Anyone could come and go, and fixers were even seen in promoters' boxes and at matches." In addition to the regression in security, the sheer numerousness of these tournaments means that a player's form is not tracked in the same way. Kevin Pietersen's form for his IPL side does not determine his place in the England T20 team; were he allowed to play in the Bangladesh or Sri Lanka Premier Leagues, his performances would not be a factor.

But, more than anything, the danger posed by these tournaments— and the cluttered cricket calendar more generally—is that the sheer volume of cricket played breeds a feeling of boredom. When there are so many games, it is impossible for each one to matter. And when there are games that feel inconsequential, underperforming in one or two of them seems less of a big deal. For example, between July 2013 and January 2014 Australia and England will play anything up to 65 days of competitive cricket against each other. Even within the oldest rivalry in cricket, it is difficult to imagine players geeing themselves up to fight each day with the utmost intensity. And if the Ashes foes cannot be relied upon to summon the energy for yet another match, what hope other series?

Put simply, for the sake of countering corruption, the calendar is an area where cricket administrators have to set an example to their players by being less avaricious. In their desire to boost revenue from broadcasting rights and gate receipts, national boards have increased the volume of limited-overs matches to such an extent that they have devalued their product. This is evidenced by the fact that national selectors are increasingly embracing rotation policies to keep their key players fit for the most important series. Coaches want to play their strongest sides in every match, but the amount of cricket scheduled means that players cannot cope with appearing in every game. The problem with rotation is that it sends an implicit message that not all matches are equal, and, as we have seen, when matches are considered less important they become vulnerable to corruption. As long ago as

2000 Gideon Haigh likened cricket's administrators to "state governments who publicly deplore the social costs of gambling, but can't get enough of fat gambling revenues". If anything, the addition of national boards to hosting cricket matches has only become more powerful in the past decade. There are many reasons why a cluttered calendar is bad for cricket, and the tacit encouragement of corruption is another.

It is impossible to tell whether, on balance, these developments will make players more or less vulnerable to corruption in the future. Grouping cricketers under the single banner of "players" is probably unhelpful—if MS Dhoni were approached by a fixer, the costs and benefits that would run through his mind are completely different to those of an average county player. It also ignores the fact that cricketers are individuals. The discussion in the South Africa dressing room in Mumbai showed the different reactions to a potential fix. Some rejected the opportunity on moral grounds, others for economic reasons, while others were interested even though it made little sense. Cronje's behaviour at Centurion, which resulted in the only Test match with a proven fixed outcome, certainly wasn't based on rational thought. The money on offer was small beans, even in the pre-IPL period, and he could have taken less of a risk by cheating in a different competition. This is an unhappy reality for cricket's anti-corruption officials. Cheating can be made as unattractive as possible, but some will still succumb.

Among the majority who do behave rationally, the best that we can aim for is to try to spot trends. Since the Cronje era, the incentive for Test cricketers to participate in match-fixing appears to be in decline. Higher wages mean that the spoils of fixing are, relatively speaking, unattractive. There is more flexibility within cricket's labour market, so, if a player is not being picked for the national team, he has the opportunity to earn a comparable salary elsewhere. The high visibility of the Test match increases the risk of being caught, suggesting that fixes are more likely to take place elsewhere. The exponential growth in T20 tournaments means that there are opportunities for players to take bribes to play badly without their apparent loss of form resulting in their being dropped from the national team. Taken together, these are good reasons for supporters of Test cricket to be confident that the matches they follow are real. They do not, however, imply that the sport as a whole is severing its links with corruption. Cricket's historical context suggests that the two will co-exist forever. However, given the difficulty of manipulating a five-day game and the easier opportunities available elsewhere, the odds on fixing in Test matches are lengthening.

If the intertwined history of cricket and gambling has told us anything, it is that the next attempted fix is not far away. There is no doubt that another case will emerge in the next three or four years. The incentives for fixers to continue to devise new schemes and the vulnerabilities of players to their approaches remain considerable. Based on what we know about previous examples and how match-fixing works, we can sketch out what it will look like.

It will be detected in England or Australia, where the security procedures are tightest and the media the most inquisitive. It will not be discovered by the authorities, although the ACSU will claim (probably correctly) that it was monitoring the individuals involved. It will come to light as a result of an overheard conversation or a misdirected text message or tweet.

There will be no more than one or two players involved, given how unwieldy fixes involving more players have proved to be. The participants will not be those in the team traditionally targeted by fixers. They could be a lower-order batsman, a bits-and-pieces spinner or a second-change bowler. They will not be in possession of an expensive IPL contract or a central contract with one of the higher-paying national boards.

The setting will not be a Test match, but nor will it be a county or state game. Instead, it is likely to be a domestic T20 tournament, where players travel from all over the world, mix with different people (making it harder for officials to monitor behaviour) and play for teams to which they have only the loosest affiliation. They will have been approached by another player in the team or by a friend or family member. There will be a trace, probably through several links, to someone who bets on cricket illegally in India or Pakistan.

The players will probably be involved in manipulating brackets, which appears to be the bet offered by South Asian bookies that is most vulnerable to corruption. However, the bet will involve some kind of twist that differentiates it from the sort of manipulation outlined earlier in the chapter. It is unlikely that the fixer will target markets for the innings runs or the match result, given that these probably require the complicity of more members of the team.

Something about the fix will go wrong. This will ensure that neither the players nor the fixer is able to defraud the bookmaker. The bookmaker might cancel the bet at the last minute or the players may not follow the fixer's instructions precisely. Either way, it will not proceed as planned.

The subsequent official investigation will ban the players involved, but will lack the scope to investigate the fixer, or how he intended the defrauding of the bookmaker to occur. As a result, the amount of new information that the authorities, the media and spectators will learn about fixing will be limited.

Chapter Six
The Broadcasters

> *"There's a little bit of the whore in all of us, gentlemen.*
> *What's your price?"*
>
> *Kerry Packer*

....

There is only one contender for the unofficial role of the father of modern cricket and his name is Kerry Packer. The hulking Australian with hands like hams and slicked-back hair left his imprint on the sport almost 40 years ago and has been in his grave for the best part of a decade, but his influence continues to be felt every time cricket appears on television. Like many of the men in the top echelons of the sport today, Packer was no cricket tragic. He boxed in his youth, and, as an older man, he fell in love with polo. But, when he inherited the struggling Nine television network from his father, Sir Frank Packer, in 1974, he soon looked to cricket to boost its ratings.

At the time, there was no such thing as a professional Australian cricketer. When he was not terrorising the world's best batsmen, Dennis Lillee moonlighted as the owner of an office-cleaning company. He had little option to look outside the sport, because the Australian Cricket Board (ACB) was satisfied with paying him A$400 (£250) a game, safe in the knowledge that, if Lillee protested, it would scarcely be short of willing replacements. Unsurprisingly, resentment in the dressing room was rife; the circumstances were set for a union movement. The players found their champion in Packer, who had become equally hacked off with the ACB. In 1976 he offered the board A$1.5m—more than seven times the usual fee that it received from the Australian Broadcasting Corporation (ABC)—for a three-year contract to broadcast domestic and international matches played in Australia. The ACB turned him down in favour of maintaining its relationship with ABC, pushing the players into Packer's arms and creating one of the most famous cricket stories of all.

Packer's World Series Cricket (WSC) shook the Test match out of a decades-long reverie and forced its administrators to confront the dilemmas of the modern sporting world. A bewildering number of innovations occurred within its two-year lifespan: night-time matches, a white ball, fielding circles, coloured clothing, drop-in pitches, cameras at both ends of the ground and microphones in the stumps. But, more than any of these, the real legacy of WSC has been the introduction of competition to the process of awarding broadcasting rights. Prior to WSC, cricket administration, if not the sport itself, had been thoroughly resistant to commercial realities. The ACB was happy to receive a fraction of what its rights were worth, keeping its players just out of penury, but also denying itself the opportunity to improve training, fitness and its own facilities.

The situation was the same in England, where the BBC paid the Test and County Cricket Board (TCCB, the precursor to the England and Wales Cricket Board or ECB) a meagre sum for Test coverage. The England captain, Tony Greig, made £210 a match in the pre-Packer age, and his major employer was his county. The national team consisted of a group of players assembled the day before a Test by the selectors and put to work for five days before going their separate ways. There was nothing in the way of support staff, no conditioning training, certainly no "informed player management". When cricket was first televised in India in the 1980s, the Board for Control of Cricket in India (BCCI) had to pay the state television broadcaster, Doordarshan, for the pleasure of screening home internationals. Cricket was selling itself short, but Packer was the only man to realise it.

In its second season, in 1978-79, WSC steamrollered the official offerings of the ACB. A weakened Australia team lost the Ashes at home to Mike Brearley's England and crowd numbers for the Australian domestic competition, the Sheffield Shield, slumped. Packer's commercial sense won out. A lavish promotional budget, a hit single ('C'mon Aussie C'mon) and a relaxation of the outdated fussiness that had clung to the sport like an old-fashioned cardigan made WSC feel fresh and exciting. It was no co-incidence that it was during WSC that women were first permitted to enter the members' area of the Sydney Cricket Ground (SCG). The ACB was exposed as being badly out of touch. Suitably humbled, in April 1979 it agreed to sell exclusive rights to international cricket in Australia to Packer for three years—and for less than he had offered in 1976. It was the start of a relationship between the ACB and Nine that continues to this day, and one that has been partly responsible for the huge success of the Australian Test team in the years since. But the contribution that Packer-led competition has made to the world game is larger still.

Before exploring how broadcasting revenue is changing Test cricket, it is important to realise that the explosion in the size of the television deals (which are now by far the biggest source of revenue in cricket) has come about without any direct involvement from the sport's governing body, the International Cricket Council (ICC). This would be unthinkable in many sports, even Premier League football, where rights are negotiated centrally. But this was never a possibility in cricket, partly because the ICC is very much undersized compared to its peers. As Gideon Haigh points out in his exposé of the inner wranglings of the organisation in *Wisden*, the ICC remains a comparatively young body, which only attained independence from the Marylebone Cricket Club (MCC) at Lord's in 1993. At this point, the ICC had a staff of four, and annual revenue was no more than £100,000. According to Haigh, "A running gag was that international cricket could afford crises only on Monday, Wednesday and Friday, because those were the days when the media manager worked." Owing to its small stature and very limited resources, the ICC would have been unable to impose itself on negotiations of television rights deals on behalf of its member boards, even if it had thought to do so.

Instead, the ICC behaves in the same way as the boards that compose it—and undertakes the same negotiations with television companies to ensure that it receives the greatest revenue that it can for its fixtures: the 50-over World Cup, the Champions Trophy, the World Twenty20 (T20) and, potentially, the finals of the World Test Championship. It was the sum of around US$550m (£350m) that the ICC managed to extract from a subsidiary of Rupert Murdoch's News Corp, Global Cricket Corporation, in 2000 for coverage of the 2003 and 2007 World Cups that elevated the ICC into something more than a dusty offshoot of the MCC. When this deal was renewed in late 2006 to cover the period up to the end of the 2015 World Cup, the ICC managed to double its money. These deals have brought the ICC into the same financial orbit as the largest national boards: the BCCI, Cricket Australia (CA, the new name for the ACB) and the ECB, but it is still not in the position to assume management of television rights deals on behalf of its members.

The institutional weakness of the ICC is only one of the threads that form the recent development of international cricket, but it is a crucial one. Owing to the liberalisation forced through by Packer, the value of broadcasting deals has grown exponentially in the past 20 years. But, as the negotiations have been conducted individually between the board and the broadcasters, rather than collectively, the revenue generated has become more and more unequal between countries. Inevitably, this had led to Test-playing nations splitting into two camps. The haves have signed broadcasting contracts worth hundreds of millions of pounds and the have-nots have not. The former group is able to exert a disproportionate influence over the global schedule (to ensure that its teams play as many lucrative matches among themselves as possible) and the teams are investing their income in coaching staff and facilities to improve their performance. The latter group is penned in, struggling with a schedule that gives its teams fewer Tests against the elite and, therefore, less of a chance to hone their skills and improve their income; they must, as a consequence, try to win matches against teams with much greater resources.

The point of this chapter is not to demonise the boards of cricket's biggest and most successful nations, but it is necessary to understand how we arrived at this state of affairs. The BCCI, CA and the ECB have done an effective job in encouraging television networks to view the rights to cricket as a valuable commodity. Importantly, the Indian and English boards were only able to make a step-change in transforming their income once they had post-Packer Packer moments of their own. In England, this came with the severing of the decades-long monopoly of the British Broadcasting Corporation (BBC). When Sky first got a look-in, in 1994, and was granted the rights to show highlights packages, the value of domestic broadcasting rights jumped from £15m for three years to £58m for four years. And the value of subsequent deals rose handsomely each time. The deals signed with Channel 4 and Sky in 1998 was worth £100m over four years; the next, £180m over three years, until, finally, they reached a plateau, with the two most recent agreements with Sky and Channel 5 bringing in £260m each over four years. A seven-year deal for the rights to show England matches in Asia was signed with ESPN Star in mid-2012, and was worth around US$200m.

In India, the rate of growth has been even faster. As recently as 1992, the Indian broadcast media was entirely closed to foreign investment, and cricket was broadcast on the state network, Doordarshan. Not only did the BCCI receive no money at all from Doordarshan, but it was expected to cover all of the broadcaster's production costs. This changed at the same time as the government chose to fight an economic slump by dismantling the protectionism of the Licence Raj regime and ushering in the first wave of foreign investment. In 1993 TransWorld International (TWI), an independent producer and distributor, approached the BCCI and bought the global rights to England's tour of India later that year for US$200,000. Andrew Wildblood, who led the negotiations for TWI, recalls the "quaint" squabbling over the last US$25,000 with the then secretary of the BCCI, Jagmohan Dalmiya and the president, IS Bindra. The sum looks laughably small today, but, at the time, it helped to convince the BCCI that there was money to be made by pursuing the opening up of the telecoms sector.

After this deal was signed, there followed several years of legal disputes between the BCCI, Doordarshan (who, according to Wildblood, felt that the broadcasts were its birthright) and prospective foreign investors, before a case found itself in front of the Supreme Court. The land's highest legal authority ruled that, "The right to impart and receive information is a species of the right to freedom of speech," and permitted the BCCI to award the coverage to whomever it wished. Immediately, the value of rights shot up, and Doordarshan found itself paying around US$50m to screen domestic Indian internationals between 2000 and 2004. The value has since continued to soar, with the most recent contract for domestic internationals in 2012-18 awarded to ESPN Star (now solely Star) for around US$700m.

There has also been big money made in South Africa, where eight-year deals for overseas rights covering 2012-20 were signed with Taj Television and Willow TV in late 2011 for Asia and the Americas, respectively, for a total of US$200m. Domestic rights are less lucrative, partly because, as in Australia, legislation demands that domestic international cricket matches are shown on free-to-air television. This has yet to prove detrimental to CA's finances, because Nine has always faced competition from other domestic broadcasters, which has kept the price of the rights high. In South Africa, however, the South Africa Broadcasting Corporation (SABC) has been beset by financial problems in recent years. As a result, Cricket South Africa (CSA) reduced the price of the rights deal for the 2012/13 season by around 50%, to US$3.5m, in order to ensure continued coverage.

Outside of India, Australia, England and, to a lesser extent, South Africa, rights have proved less valuable, as demographics, prosperity and cricket's place in the sporting pecking order are less favourable. Furthermore, what money the national boards receive is earned through selling international, rather than domestic, rights. Local audiences for Test cricket in New Zealand, the West Indies and Sri Lanka, in particular, are so small that domestic rights are effectively zero as an income stream, which is a huge handicap, given that India, England and Australia earn hundreds of millions of dollars from their home markets. Among the international deals, New Zealand Cricket (NZC) sold rights for overseas broadcasting of international games for eight years to Pitch International, effectively a middle-man operation that repackages rights and sells them on, for around US$100m in April 2012. At the time of writing, Sri Lanka Cricket (SLC) was weighing up multiple offers for overseas rights to domestic international cricket for a seven-year period, but none is believed to be over US$60m. The West Indies Cricket Board (WICB) did not disclose the size of the seven-year deal that it signed with Taj TV for overseas rights in late 2012, but it is likely to be similar to the previous two. In Bangladesh, an attempt in 2012 to sell international rights to domestic cricket for US$15m failed to attract serious interest, and the Bangladesh Cricket Board (BCB) has since reverted to selling rights on a series-by-series basis.

The differences, then, between the haves and the have-nots are huge. The BCCI is able to pull in over US$100m a year from its domestic rights deal, which is around the same as NZC was able to raise for eight years of overseas coverage. The chief executive of the New Zealand Cricket Players Association (NZCPA), Heath Mills, put it like this to *The New Zealand Herald*: "We can never have a level playing field again. We're talking 1.2bn people versus 4.5m. We're talking US$250m versus US$40m revenue. That's okay in a largely amateur sport like rowing, because countries are spending a similar amount on high performance. In cricket, there's huge disparity in the high-performance spend." Given the two boards' relative spending power, it is a surprise, purely from an economic perspective, that New Zealand were able to hold England to three drawn Tests during their home series in February and March 2013.

However, this series was an anomaly, as the trend of results in Test cricket runs overwhelmingly in the direction of a two-tier system, where the big four nations play competitive series among themselves, but steamroller the rest. New Zealand have not won a series, home or away, against any of India, Australia, England or South Africa since 2002. The West Indies beat England at home in 2009, but, before that, their previous win anywhere was in 1998. Sri Lanka won home series against South Africa in 2006, England in 2007 and India in 2008, but have not won any since the retirement of their talismanic offspinner, Muttiah Muralitharan. Pakistan beat England in the Middle East in 2012, but their previous success was at home to India in 2006. Bangladesh have never won a series against these teams. At a time when Test cricket should be becoming more competitive, and teams such as Sri Lanka and Bangladesh should be reaping the rewards of greater experience, the performances of the have-nots are going backwards.

And it is being noticed. I spoke to one of Australia's most prominent cricket journalists, Malcolm Conn, in Sydney and asked him to name the biggest problem facing Test cricket. He replied without missing a beat:

"There is far too much junk cricket. The only thing that administrators seem to be interested in, particularly those on the subcontinent, is money, and the easiest way to make money is to schedule matches, so they keep playing more and more. The only way that most countries can make money, including Australia, is to have India tour so that they can sell the television rights back to India. That's how international cricket survives... Zimbabwe is not a real Test nation. Bangladesh is not a real Test nation. New Zealand is barely a real Test nation. There needs to be a sanctity about Test cricket and some sort of qualifying criteria."

Conn is right—a visit from India is the most important event in the calendar (with the exception of the Ashes) for any cricketing nation—but his prescription for what to do about it is entirely wrong. Cricket should not be responding to a slew of one-sided series by retrenching. Although the financial incentives (or, rather, disincentives) are there for the haves to cut the number of matches that they play against the have-nots, to do so would be an act of self-sabotage, for several reasons.

First, cricket is a game that has always and unambiguously benefited from diversity. Test cricket is different in each of the countries in which it is played, and it is a richer game for it. To be a great Test match cricketer is to master the conditions in Pallekele, Port-of-Spain and Perth, and to watch cricket in environments as different as these is part of the education of following the sport. Second, to follow Conn's suggestion of weaker teams playing qualifiers among themselves for the right to play the bigger teams is to deliver a firm slap in the face of the progress that has been made in Sri Lanka and Bangladesh in the past 30 years. And how is cricket in the Caribbean, faced with greater competition from other sports than ever before, supposed to match its former glories if its current players are denied the chance to compete against the best? If the sport that is served up is perceived to be second-rate, it will fail to hold the attention of the fans. The editor of *The New Zealand Herald*, Shayne Currie, says, "If the Black Caps win like they did in Hobart [against Australia] last year, it will always be front-page news, but, unfortunately, those moments are few and far between and the public wants more than wins against Zimbabwe and Bangladesh and even Sri Lanka". Third, and most simply, it sends out the wrong message. What sporting administrator can say that they are doing their best for their sport if they respond ambivalently to the idea of restricting access to it? Cricket is a growing sport, and should be treated as such.

Yet not only is there growing support for a "two-tier" system as a method to make Test cricket more competitive, but there is evidence from the schedule that it is already happening. As of April 2013, 16 of England's last 30 Tests have been against India, Australia or South Africa, as are 10 of the next 12. Of India's last 30 Tests, 19 have been against the other three biggest nations, while the figure is 18 out of 30 for Australia. The numbers are similar for the West Indies (17/30) and New Zealand (17/30), but the difference is that England and Australia have played those 30 matches in a little over two years, whereas it has taken New Zealand and the West Indies almost four. The big teams are already playing each other most frequently and over longer series. Priority is already given to the premier series in the calendar; there is no need to denigrate the poorer nations further.

In fact, if anything, more opportunities should be given to the have-nots. Despite living next-door to the sole cricketing superpower, Bangladesh have never played a Test in India and only twice have they played a series of three Tests. Their cricketers are being set a remarkably stiff challenge: prove your worth to the calendar, but without the experience needed to do so. Likewise, the whole of the cricket world is hoping for a renaissance in the West Indies, but the team must achieve it while playing Test series of three matches or fewer. For all that Sri Lanka is now an accepted part of the cricket world, Test match cricket's highest wicket-taker of them all, Murali, never played a four-match series. This is not to suggest that England need to play five-Test series with Bangladesh every other year, but it is disingenuous to suggest that the solution to uncompetitive, "junk" cricket is for the biggest sides to play each other more often, thereby ensuring that they receive an even bigger slice of the broadcasting pie.

It is impossible to conceive of a situation where the national boards get together, either under the guise of the ICC, or independently, and decide that, for the future health and growth of the game, broad-casting revenue should be negotiated centrally and/or divided more equitably. For one thing, the BCCI, the ECB, CA and CSA require more revenue, as they have larger infrastructures to maintain. Unlike other sports, most notably football, where players are contracted to their clubs and "loaned" to international teams for short periods of time, in cricket international players are now usually contracted to their country, for which they make the majority of their appearances. This has had the effect of taking the star attractions away from the county or state leagues, and with them much of the attention that those leagues need to survive. As a result, they have long been subsidised by the national boards.

The TCCB used to act exactly like a clearinghouse. From its total revenue, the cost of running the international team, administration of the domestic league and staff salaries were subtracted and whatever was left over was divided more or less equally between the counties. This reflected the fact that national boards were dependent upon the counties (or states) to find, train and develop the cricketers that went on to represent the country in internationals. The ECB's accounts have since become a little more complicated as its revenue has risen (a decent proportion of its revenue is now also spent on promoting cricket at "grassroots" level), but the principle of disbursing revenue to the counties remains the same. In 2011 the 18 teams in the English County Championship received £42.5m, out of a total expenditure of £117m. The ECB refers to the counties as centres of excellence; in effect, they have become the breeding grounds for the Test cricketers of the future. And, in the bigger countries, the architecture of state or county cricket is that much larger and requires greater revenue to sustain it.

There are also those, such as IMG's Andrew Wildblood, who are of the view that, although the big four receive the lion's share of the broadcasting revenue, they are already fulfilling their responsibility to ensure it is shared more equitably, by touring. He explains: "Those national boards with weak domestic media markets are sustained at least in part by revenue from the Indian market. So, by playing against those countries, it can be argued that the BCCI gives other boards the opportunity to access the riches of the Indian market." Wildblood's point is that the WICB earns more money from selling the rights to an Indian tour of the Caribbean back to India than it does to viewers in the Caribbean; therefore, the BCCI is helping to generate revenue for other boards. I find this an overly charitable view, given that the BCCI also needs India to play in order to generate its own revenue. However, it remains an argument that the big four could fall back on, if their position of financial dominance were ever questioned.

It is clear that any hope of a system being adopted that divides up revenue from television rights more equitably should be abandoned right here. The current get-what-you-can model has been in place for too long now for any new scheme to be tolerated and the ICC is too weak to intervene, even if it were spoiling for a fight.[1]

....

1   A revenue-sharing model was proposed by Boston Consulting Group, which was hired to look into the future of Test cricket by CA in 2008, but the suggestion was rejected by the BCCI and the ECB. Instead, the most notable scheme that exists is the ICC's Targeted Assistance and Performance Programme (TAPP), which was introduced in 2012 with a fund of US$12m. Resources are made available to full ICC members at the bottom of the rankings, and to the bigger associate members, to help to improve team performance. In 2013 it was announced that NZC had received US$1.8m to finance a New Zealand "A" team. It is a laudable gesture, and represents the acknowledgement that cricket's rich should help the poor, but, in the context of the size of some television-rights deals, the TAPP is small beer.

But that does not mean that the main implication of this system—a gradual slide into two-tier cricket with an ever-shrinking number of competitive teams—is guaranteed. There is a new frontier within broadcasting that could come to rival or even surpass television in the revenue that it generates. It is more flexible than TV and the devices that it requires are already on the market. All that needs to be implemented is the infrastructure. Most excitingly of all, the way in which its rights are distributed is still to be decided. The new frontier is the Internet.

Back in 2000, when the first wave of excitement about the Internet was at its peak, the owner of the Chicago White Sox baseball team, Jerry Reinsdorf, met the then president of Major League Baseball (MLB), Paul Beeston, in New York and the pair discussed their mutual concern that the Internet would widen the "economic gap" between the league's bigger and smaller teams, and, by doing so, reduce the competitiveness of MLB. Reinsdorf and Beeston then took a proposal to the MLB commissioner, Bud Selig, asking for the creation of a centralised web portal for all of the league's teams, and that any revenue generated from it—from merchandise or watching games online–be shared equally. Selig put it to the teams, who, after several months of deliberating, approved it. The decision was perhaps made easier by the fact that there was no guarantee that it would earn any money at all. At the time, the Internet seemed full of possibilities, but no-one really knew what they were.

One man who had a firmer idea than most was Bob Bowman, the man whom Selig brought in to manage the project. Bowman is one of those people who are three steps ahead of everyone else and spends their time solving problems before others realise that the problems exist. He had a stint at Goldman Sachs as an investment banker before becoming state treasurer of Michigan before he was 30. After a change of administration in the state in 1990, Bowman left to become chief financial officer of Sheraton Hotels, before moving on up to run the chain's parent company, ITT. He left in 1998 and went looking for a new challenge. Soon after, Selig was in touch, Bowman came on board and Major League Baseball Advanced Media (BAM) was born. There was a happy symmetry to the partnership: in 1970 Selig bought a bankrupt baseball team in Seattle and shifted it eastwards to become the Milwaukee Brewers. Bowman, who was 11 at the time, lived nearby and became a die-hard Brewers fan. He remembers seeing Selig pacing around above him in the owners' box.

Bowman quickly saw the potential of BAM, and the importance of doing it right. "Baseball was the first [sport] to be on radio, the first to be on TV, on cable, and now digital media," he told Chuck Salter. "Think back to 1950 when the three sports that mattered were baseball, boxing and horse racing. Two of them disappeared. Not baseball." He announced that BAM could generate revenue of US$600m in ten years, a hefty sum even in that age of endless optimism about the Internet. As it happened, the noughties were bookended by the tech crunch of 2001 and the global financial crisis of 2008-09. Despite these shocks, BAM reached its target, only a year behind schedule.

Bowman set about his task with zeal, persuading each of the league's 30 owners to put in combined seed money of US$77m. The first couple of years were choppy. Most users were accessing the site on slow dial-up connections and it took until August 2002 before BAM felt confident enough in their broadcasting capabilities to dare show a game live. Nevertheless, the firm was amassing a group of paying subscribers, a rare thing at a time before paywalls and pay-per-view models began to limit access. As the technology improved, both in homes and in the BAM headquarters in Manhattan, the subscriber base began to grow and the quality of the broadcasts improved. BAM added more cameras within the stadiums and allowed viewers to switch between them. Long before Sky+, they introduced pause, rewind and fast-forward functions. Stats and visuals could be called up at the push of a button. Watching a baseball game on MLB.com was not the same as watching it passively on television. It was more like being the director of the broadcast in the studio.

The next milestone for BAM was the launch of AtBat, its iPhone app, in July 2008. (It is a measure of how quickly BAM jumps onto new technology that AtBat was launched on the same day as Apple's

App Store.) Apple takes a 30% cut from sales through the App Store, so BAM had to sell a high volume to maintain profitability. As with the immediate construction of a paywall in 2001, the decision to get involved with Apple was another Bowman hunch that proved spot-on. AtBat was the highest-grossing app in the entire store in 2011. It is free to download, but access to live content costs US$15 a year for audio and US$120 a year for video. The launch of the iPad app two years later pushed the number of subscribers up further, and by 2011 the total stood at 2.2m and was growing at 25% a year, with a renewal rate of 85%. Annual revenue has long exceeded Bowman's initial target of US$600m.

More recent innovations include an app for Microsoft's Xbox with an archive of past matches that can be viewed through your HD television and a highlights mode that allows you to filter the type of action that you want to see, such as home runs, strikes out or catches. For the current, 2013 season, BAM also started streaming spring training matches.

For all that BAM has offered a richer, more interactive and more convenient way to watch baseball, there are still tensions that have necessitated compromises. The sole serious concern from the owners when the idea of BAM was floated was that it would steal viewers away from television, compromising the league's existing rights deals, which are worth more than US$2bn a year. (A bit more, but in the same ballpark, as those for cricket.) The fudge is that local games are blacked out in the immediate vicinity, in order to protect the size of the TV audience. So far, three teams have chosen to permit so-called in-market streaming, but audiences have remained fairly small. Bowman told *The New York Times* that the effect of BAM on television has been benign: "We've learned that, wherever you are, you watch on the biggest screen you can." This makes sense; you wouldn't choose to watch a game at home on your four-inch iPhone screen when you have a 60-inch television in the living room, but, if you were on the train, you'd choose your phone or tablet over nothing at all. This is why Bowman claims that much of the revenue that BAM generates is new, rather than poached from television or from the stadiums. In 2011 for the first time the majority of BAM's traffic came from mobile devices, a fact that supports Bowman's argument.

BAM's relationship with the going-to-the-game ritual is interesting.

One would assume that BAM would like there to be just enough fans to fill the stadiums and generate a good atmosphere, and for everyone else to stream the game from home. But this doesn't appear to be true. Baseball is still a game economy, rather than a broadcast economy. Unlike cricket, most of its revenue is generated around its stadiums, through tickets, merchandise and food and drink. BAM spent time researching fan behaviour and generated a new app, called At the Ballpark. This allows fans to buy tickets to matches digitally, share their locations with other fans through social media and order food and drink to their seats. The details of purchasers stored in its online database means that it can target fans with promotions and offer loyalty discounts. So convinced is BAM of the importance of getting fans to the game that it spent US$10m installing digital kiosks at ballparks across the US.

It is here that this model begins to look seriously exciting for fans of Test cricket. A new and lucrative form of income that is spread equitably between the different nations would help the smaller teams develop the kind of resources that the big four now take for granted. Heath Mills of the NZCPA recently lamented, "New Zealand remains the most under-resourced team in world cricket. Teams like Australia, England, South Africa and India have twice the staff... As long as that continues, every other team in the world will continue to get better than us." With another, steady form of income, NZC can begin to narrow that gap. In addition, if cricket's authorities borrowed the same idea to use digital media to encourage fans through the gate, it could address another of Test cricket's familiar failings: falling attendances. There is no reason to believe that the methods used to entice Americans to baseball would be any less successful in getting West Indians or South Africans to cricket, and if Test cricket shows it is capable of communicating to a younger audience through new technology, there is no reason to believe that interest will not be reciprocated.

Then, there is the product itself: MLB.tv and AtBat are seriously nice pieces of design. To flick between the myriad options within Game Day mode, where numerous live stats and tables can be picked up and put down, feels like an innovation that should be available to cricket. In the past ten years, Sky, in particular, has been innovative in bringing new technology and graphics to its cricket coverage. But the next step is to employ BAM's customisation and let viewers choose their camera angle, pull up a wagon wheel or a HawkEye projection. And if any group of people would be prepared to pay for this level of anorakary, it is fans of Test cricket.

It is also clear that cricket is crying out for a centralised online archive of footage. In recent years, a hugely dedicated Australian man, Rob Moody, who describes himself as a "100% insane cricket nerd", has built an entirely unofficial YouTube channel containing over 2,000 short clips of cricket highlights. His archive is clearly filling a gap in the market: a two-and-a-half minute video of Tasmania's David Saker felling Jeff Vaughan of South Australia with a vicious bouncer has been viewed almost 2 million times. Now imagine the same archive, with a slick interface, remastered content and accessible at any time on a phone, tablet, laptop or computer. It has enormous potential. Want to watch India vs Australia from Calcutta in 2001 over again? Just load it up. Or Edgbaston 2005? Or all 1,438 balls faced by Alastair Cook in the 2010/11 Ashes? Settle down and tuck in.

Baseball and cricket have moved in lock-step in the past century. The first baseball game to be broadcast on the radio took place in 1921. Cricket followed a year later, when Charles Bannerman's testimonial at the SCG was aired. The first Test match to be shown on television was in 1938, when England's Wally Hammond and Australia's Sir Donald Bradman traded centuries in a drawn game at Lord's. Baseball followed 14 months later, when the New York area was shown a match between the Brooklyn Dodgers and the Cincinnati Reds. However, baseball has left cricket behind when it comes to digital. From the UK, it is possible to watch all cricket matches shown on Sky Sports through an iPhone app, but it lacks AtBat's functionality. And the rest of the world's cricket, which is not shown by Sky? Forget it.

But there are some serious obstacles that would have to be overcome before cricket fans are able to tap the same resources as subscribers to BAM. I put the idea of a cricket AtBat to Andrew Wildblood, who doubts that digital platforms could attract new fans, and so would risk cannibalising existing television rights deals. "If you want to watch the Test match, you don't care whether you watch it on an iPhone or on television. You aren't going to suddenly become a cricket fan because of the digital offering. However, existing fans will choose to access the content on a variety of platforms, and in time this could have a positive effect on broadcasters' revenue."

BAM sees it slightly differently. It believes that the three main ways of watching baseball—at the stadium, on television and on the web—do not operate in the largely zero-sum situation that Wildbood describes. It argues that, if fans enjoy their day out at the game, they are likely to watch more baseball at home and to buy AtBat to catch up while travelling. Similarly, if the coverage of baseball on television is interesting and innovative, fans are more likely to want to watch more ballgames, and so are more likely to take on a subscription for their phone or tablet. This is a brave stance, because, once you've introduced a product like AtBat, the genie won't go back in the bottle. However, the baseball teams that have taken the risk and permitted streaming of their games in their local areas, such as the New York Yankees and the San Diego Padres, have not seen their attendances fall. This suggests the zero-sum model is wrong, and that sports can attract new followers by reaching out to different demographics in different ways.

In addition to concerns about the size of the market is the fact that cricket's administrators have no track record on the kind of co-operation that would be necessary. Here's Bill Schlough, chief information officer of the San Francisco Giants, talking about friction between MLB teams and baseball's administrators to Chuck Salter: "We have our fights now and then. It's just the way it is. We have to recognise that we're a one-thirtieth owner in this entity and we have to respect each other." Now imagine those words coming from the president of the BCCI, N Srinivasan. Difficult, eh? The comparison between baseball and cricket is not an entirely fair one, of course. The MLB is a single league, played in a single country, operating under a single legal jurisdiction. All of its members are (roughly) pulling in the same direction. But, even allowing for the social, cultural, political and historic differences between the cricket-playing nations (and there is a definite sense that Asia is enjoying its moment in the sun after decades of Anglo-Australian dominance), too many administrators lack the spirit of working together for the good of the game. The atmosphere surrounding ICC summits is somewhere between frosty and confrontational, rather than convivial and collaborative.

The ICC is only as effective as each of its members is committed. Every permanent member appoints a representative to its board of directors, the main decision-making body. Although this approach has the veneer of democracy and stability, it also leaves the ICC powerless to affect the individuals that compose it. As Gideon Haigh argues, "Unless well supervised and suitably motivated, the representatives themselves will tend to create not a genuine forum for policymaking, but an arena of competing sectional interests, prioritising the extraction of short-term benefits for those who have chosen them over the long-term welfare of the body on which they sit, and standing solidly in defence of the status quo, because reform will involve some people sacrificing hard-won eminence."

The ICC also has no influence on how each of its members chooses their representative. In several member countries, particularly in South Asia, the process is highly politicised. This leads to appointments such as that of Sharad Pawar, who became the ICC's vice-president in 2008 (and president in 2010) at the same time as he was minister of agriculture and food in the Indian government. Neither role, were he doing it properly, common sense suggests, ought to have left Pawar with much spare time. Haigh has also questioned the process that appointed Ijaz Butt as Pakistan's representative to the ICC, noting his personal connection to the then president, Asif Ali Zardari. The point is that the ICC is a hostage to the appointment processes of its member boards, and, where these processes are political, the appointees arrive at the ICC with supporters to whom they owe a favour. This leads to their serving their paymasters at home ahead of the sport they have been chosen to manage.

In contrast with the attitude of Schlough and his peers, the ICC's board of directors has failed to reach consensus in recent years, even on such basic tasks as electing a president. CA's nomination of a former Australian prime minister, John Howard, was rejected in 2010. The official reason given by the ICC was that Howard "did not have sufficient support in the ICC board", which sounds less like a reason and more like stating the obvious. The subtext is that his criticism of Zimbabwe president, Robert Mugabe, while in political office drew objections from the Zimbabwean and South African camps, while the Sri Lankan representative took umbrage to off-the-cuff remarks Howard had supposedly made about the bowling action of Muttiah Muralitharan. Neither objection had anything to do with Howard's ability to be an effective president.

More complex tasks, such as achieving consensus on the use

of technology, have fallen flat. The weakness of the ICC board of directors, and the prevailing mood of niggly opposition, rather than constructive negotiation, has produced the unhappy situation where some Tests are played with the Umpire Decision Review System (DRS) and some are not (see "The Technology" chapter). The whole sport is being held hostage on the issue by the intransigence of the BCCI. For as long as comparatively simple issues such as the DRS leave the ICC at loggerheads, the prospect of developing an innovative platform for broadcasting Tests on the net and splitting the revenue remains remote.

But perhaps the creation of an online platform for cricket streaming should fall outside of the remit of the ICC anyway. The Indian Premier League (IPL) has shown how it is possible for the private sector to shake up the sport without any involvement of the governing body. And, for all that BAM received the support of Bud Selig, it remains a separate entity from the league itself, with its own Manhattan address and its own profit and loss. Bowman answers not to Selig or the MLB itself, but to a board of team owners. As Chuck Salter argues in his profile of the firm, "Without question, BAM's success stems in part from its autonomy." There is only one company currently in existence with the brand, and possibly the ambition, to become cricket's BAM, and that is Cricinfo.

The genesis of Cricinfo is worthy of an essay in itself, but it began in 1993 as a simple programme run by a fellow at the University of Minnesota in the US to keep cricket-starved fans in the Midwest up to date with the latest scores. Twenty years later, there is live ball-by-ball commentary on all international (and some domestic) cricket, a huge array of blogs run by freelancers and the famed Statsguru database of matches and players, from which I have taken most of the numbers used in this book. It was bought by the Disney-owned powerhouse ESPN in 2007 for a fee believed to be in excess of £30m. On big match days (of which there are more and more each year), it attracts upwards of 2 million views. It is so far ahead of other cricket websites that it effectively has no competition. But it has yet to break into live streaming in the manner of BAM.

Cricinfo's was the first website to stream cricket live over the Internet, when it broadcast matches from a one-day tournament in Sharjah, the Coca-Cola Cup, in 1998. (The money to buy the

Internet rights was put up by Mick Jagger.) However, these streams were more an attempt to see what was technologically possible than the launch of a viable business model, as the site has broadcast no regular live cricket since. A company insider explained that the biggest impediment to such a development is that international boards charge so much for digital rights that "to monetise them is almost impossible". The high price is partly a consequence of the zero-sum mindset. If digital rights are perceived as a threat to television deals, which provide the bulk of the revenue that keeps the game afloat, boards will want to charge as high a price as possible to insulate themselves from a drop in television takings.

The failure of the BCCI to sell digital rights to home internationals in 2011 seems to bear this out. The board began by offering rights to matches at a base price of Rs3 crore (US$600,000) each, but this proved too high to draw out an acceptable bid. It tried again, by lowering the price to Rs2 crore, but this was also deemed too expensive. A high price could be justified if the broadcaster felt that it would recoup its outlay through revenue but, in India at least, very cheap satellite television and sluggish Internet speeds mean that the market in 2013 is small. A smaller market would mean that a broadcaster would become more dependent on advertising, through banner ads and the like, which would diminish the viewing experience. These are two fairly high barriers to entry that would require a substantial initial investment and a willingness to run a potential loss until enough subscribers are attracted by the excellence of the product.

As alternatives to India, more straightforward initial markets for the launch of such a platform are those with a substantial number of high-speed broadband connections and—conceding that there will be some migration from television to digital—expensive satellite television subscriptions. The two countries that fit this model are the UK and the US. There is no live international cricket on free-to-air television in the UK, while the concept of streaming live sport over the Internet and onto mobile devices is well established, owing to platforms such as the BBC iPlayer and Sky Go. The US—which drives a significant chunk of Cricinfo's traffic because of its large South Asian diaspora—is in a similar position. There is potential too, in Australia. Although federal legislation insists that home internationals be shown on free-to-air television, the ongoing roll-out of the country's high-speed National Broadband Network will result in a greater engagement with digital as a way to watch sport and entertainment in the next decade.

I put the idea of a cricket version of AtBat to Giles Clarke, chairman of the ECB, and to an official at CA, who spoke in a personal capacity and wished to remain anonymous. For such a platform to be brought to market, the involvement of the national boards would be essential, as they are the holders of future rights, and of the archives of footage filmed during previous domestic internationals. Both Clarke and my contact at CA identified the cumbersome negotiations that would be required in order to purchase the rights from each individual board as a difficult hurdle to jump. The CA representative stressed the co-operation that would be required in bringing all the boards' rights deals into alignment so that a single buyer could scoop them up, and the likelihood that politics would intervene at some stage to wreck the deal.

Yet Clarke was enthusiastic about the existence of demand, telling me that, "Cricket punters are very similar to baseball punters. People absolutely love stats, and they love dredging up footage from the past." He was also dismissive of the idea that such a platform would weaken future television deals. "During the last hour of the Auckland Test between England and New Zealand [in March 2013, when the tourists were nine wickets down and held on for a thrilling draw to leave the series also drawn, 0-0] New Zealand television had record viewing figures. Around one-third of the population was watching. But how many more would it have been if you didn't have to be near a TV? I heard tales of 60 people round a single screen in an office. Imagine if they all had the cricket streaming on their devices."

Clarke also offered up a new idea, of signing an exclusive deal with a telecoms company, such as Samsung or Apple, to stream a particular series through a single range of products. Were Apple to buy exclusive digital rights to streams of India's next trip to England in 2014, the firm wouldn't have to sell too many new iPhones in India to make a profit, and the ECB could gain a further few hundred million pounds. But this approach, which is more straightforward and more readily profitable than the centralised model, is also built on the opposite philosophy to that which has seen BAM become so successful. AtBat is available across as many phones and tablets as BAM has been able to write code for, as well as on computers and games consoles. The whole point is to make baseball accessible and to drive attendances at grounds, as well as at home. Offering exclusivity to owners of particular devices would draw out greater revenue for the particular national board, but it would do little to increase the popularity of cricket in either country. Moreover, it would further widen the existing disparity between the financial resources of Test-playing nations. The ECB and the BCCI would become richer still in comparison to NZC and WICB. The opportunity for digital rights to restore greater competition to Test cricket would be lost.

However, the logistical ease of each country's (and the ICC's) selling their rights individually means that this remains by far the more likely path for the development of digital rights to follow. As a result, the sums that the boards will raise for their rights and the products that they will each be able to develop will be a shadow of what could be produced collectively, as BAM has demonstrated. What Test cricket needs at this juncture is its very own Bob Bowman, a tech-savvy evangelist to put an arm around each of the national boards and offer some words of encouragement that the collective model could work. My research has led me to believe that the momentum around digital rights is starting to stir—Clarke was keen to tell me about a deal struck to broadcast the 2013 Ashes over the Internet to mainland Europe—but Test cricket as a whole will only benefit if the new revenue is distributed fairly. This may never happen, but, if it is going to, the plans need to be drawn up soon.

And, in the meantime, the best thing that cricket fans can do for the sport is to turn out and support the little guys. Part of the charm of Test cricket is that the thrills and spills are not meted out predictably. The portents were not great for the crowds that took a punt on the final day of the Auckland Test between England and New Zealand in March 2013. England were 90-4, and, having batted poorly for most of the series, the odds were that play was unlikely to last the day. Instead, the spectators were rewarded with a day of sport that they will never forget, as Matt Prior led one of the great rearguard actions and England squeaked a draw. But it is unreasonable to expect New Zealand to continue to contribute to such entertaining Test cricket with one hand tied behind their backs. So, until the ICC and the national boards find a way, through digital rights or otherwise, to play Test cricket on a more level field, the best chance the game has is for its fans to support its have-nots.

Saving The Test
Conclusion

*"The beauty of a Test match is that it can be enjoyed in
several ways: in its majestic fullness, over five long days;
in a short session; in a duel between batsman and bowler;
or in the action of a second. The experience is unlike any
other, at once meditative and exhilarating."*

Sambit Bal

. . . .

One of the most enjoyable conversations that I had while writing
Saving the Test was with the former Kent, Middlesex and England
batsman turned author and broadcaster, Ed Smith. A thoughtful man
with a double-first from Cambridge, Ed has the gift of seeing cricket
in its context, as one sport among many competing for attention
and resources. As such, he does not take the future health of the
Test match for granted. After finding ourselves in happy agreement
about the need for faster, bouncier Test pitches and the wisdom of
choosing appropriately sized grounds for matches, we found we were
completely opposed on the subject of scoring rates.

We concurred that the aggressive approach to batting pioneered by
Steve Waugh's Australians in the 1990s had made Test cricket more
exciting. (Waugh's tactic was so influential that the average number
of runs per over rose to 3.2 in the 2000s, from 2.86 in the 1980s.)
But our opinions diverged when Ed said he would be ambivalent
if the scoring rate went up to six or eight runs an over. I protested,
arguing that such a rate would marginalise the defensive skills that
are a crucial part of the armoury of any great Test cricketer. He
was incredulous that, in order to improve the health of the Test
match I would "protect the leave" and described me, deliberately
unflatteringly, as a cricket conservative.

I disagreed with Ed that day, and I still do. I am not a dyed-in-the-
wool traditionalist, the sort for whom anything more than 2.5 runs
an over is just not cricket. But I fear that allowing the temperature
of batting to be raised to the extent that Ed suggested would be to
permit the end of the balance between bat and ball that makes Test
cricket the extraordinary spectacle that it can be. Most people think
that the way to win a cricket match is to score more runs than the
other team. But, to no lesser extent, games are won by the team

that takes all the opposition's wickets. Too often in Twenty20 (T20) cricket, bowling feels like nothing more than serving the ball up for the master-blasting of men like Chris Gayle and Rohit Sharma. Were runs similarly easy to come by in Test cricket, the number of youngsters queuing up to become bowlers would shrink year on year. Cricket is not just a contest between two sets of batsmen, but a series of individual battles between bowlers and batsmen.

The leave, I proposed to Ed, is not a sign of a dull day's play, but evidence that the match is in the balance. When the ball passes the bat and is taken by the wicketkeeper, the bowler has failed to take the batsman's wicket and the batsman has been unable to muster a scoring shot. Were this to continue *ad infinitum* the game would become insufferably boring. Except that it never does. Someone's patience always runs out. The bowler bends his back and bowls too short or the batsman swings at a ball that is not there to hit, and the spell is broken. But some of the most thrilling spells of Test cricket take place when a match, or even a series, are at stake and neither the batsman nor the bowler is willing to give an inch. In these moments, the scoring rate is irrelevant, it is purely a battle of wills to see whether the batsman can survive or the bowler can take his wicket.

There is ample evidence of this. To my mind, there has been no better hour of Test cricket in recent years than that which took place in January 2010 during the Third Test at Newlands between South Africa and England. The hosts had a lead of just 18 after the first two innings, but a superb, fluent 183 from Graeme Smith, ably supported by Hashim Amla and Jacques Kallis, took South Africa to a declaration, having scored 447-7. On the final day, only a South African victory or a draw were possible, and by lunch England were deep in the malodorous stuff, at 179-5.

Soon afterwards, Smith took the new ball and tossed it to Dale Steyn, the best fast bowler of his generation. The six-over spell that Steyn bowled to Paul Collingwood and Ian Bell (although of the 36 balls, Collingwood faced 29) was nothing short of ferocious, a potent combination of naked aggression and supreme control. His first two overs cost 13, an unflattering statistic that disguises the fact that the batsmen could do nothing more than edge the ball through the slips or past Mark Boucher's gloves. After that, they couldn't get the bat anywhere close to the ball, which was delivered on a beautiful,

McGrathian line, inches outside of off stump. After pitching, it was moving in both directions off the seam, three deliveries shifting outwards, then one cutting back towards the batsman, forcing him to thrust the bat in ungainly fashion across his body to protect middle stump.

Collingwood, as he recalled afterwards, quickly retreated into his shell: "The first over was strange, because I thought I could score off him. Then a bit of lacquer came off and there was more seam movement than anything else and, as you could see, I couldn't lay bat on it." With each ball that shot past the stumps, the angle of Collingwood's back-lift got lower and lower, until it disappeared almost entirely. It was a superb test of mental strength, as well as technique, to pad up and protect his wicket again and again, when in each over two or three balls were defeating him. But Collingwood saw Steyn off after those six overs. Both men were exhausted. With characteristic understatement, Smith was heard to thank his bowler for "a great stint" at the end of his spell. It was so much more than that.

In the first 12 overs of the new ball, England squeaked 25 runs, a scoring rate that would have many contemporary cricket fans weeping. Yet when Collingwood correctly allowed the ball to pass his bat, there was no way that his leaves could be described as boring. They demonstrated excellent judgement in the most difficult of circumstances, and resulted in an hour of play that would have had any cricket fan in thrall. For me, Collingwood's use of the leave was indicative that everything in the Newlands Test, and indeed in that series, was as it should be. There was a lively pitch, a sufficiently long tour to build up a narrative with rivalries and sub-plots, and two sets of players that were attuned to the conditions and had a palpable will to win. It was Test cricket that felt like an event.

To bring together all of these elements, to give Test cricket a chance to thrive against its many sporting and non-sporting competitors, requires some ideological flexibility. To throw your lot in with the conservative camp (as Ed accused me of doing) and stand in rigid, unblinking opposition to T20, the Indian Premier League (IPL), bigger bats and Chris Gayle is to absent yourself from reality. But so is to surrender entirely to the other side, to that of the economic liberals who argue that cricket will exist in whatever form the market demands. Here is why both approaches are wrong, and Test cricket requires a more nuanced approach.

The IPL, which encapsulates all that cricket's conservatives abhor, is an overly long, only sporadically entertaining tournament that tries to turn a leisurely, unglamorous game into something glitzy and hedonistic. However, it has also done more than any ICC guideline or recommendation to make sure that cricket remains an obsession for a new generation in India, and a generation that is more numerous and wealthy than any before it. There is no risk of cricket becoming anachronistic in by far its most important nation while the IPL—and T20 more broadly—remain the biggest show in town. Traditionalists can then simply ignore the shortest form of the game. But those charged with running the sport have to think more carefully. The tournament should be fenced off by the ICC from the rest of the international calendar. First, it merits exclusivity, as the only annual cricket tournament of global significance. Second, Test cricket does not benefit from being cast in opposition to it. Players should not be made to resent Test cricket, nor should fans be sold a diet of matches consisting of patched-up, second-rate teams, selected from those players unable to secure an IPL contract. In return, the IPL should do its bit to encourage first-class cricket, perhaps through subsidising wages for top-performing players in the Ranji Trophy.

The trouble with the *laissez-faire* attitude to cricket's future is that the information that the market offers is incomplete, and subject to misinterpretation. The market tells us that the IPL's mix of sixes and celebrities is a winner, and that Test matches at Chester-le-Street in April are not. But that does not mean that Test cricket in England is in trouble, only that it should be played in the summer and at grounds near big cities. Likewise, it does not mean that there is endless capacity for other, derivative T20 tournaments. Cricket and its administrators are perennially accused of living in the past, yet it is cricket's traditions and history that give the game its context and richness.

During the course of this book, I have tried to outline the areas of contention in the environment in which Test cricket is played. The sport itself is not broken—Steyn's mesmeric spell to Collingwood was in all likelihood just as captivating in 2010 as Harold Larwood's to Bill Woodfull in Adelaide in 1933—but so much more can be done to encourage further Test cricket in this vein. This book is intended to encourage a more pragmatic way of thinking about the future of cricket, rather than provide a prescriptive to-do list for the authorities, but here are five straightforward recommendations to reshape the environment to be more conducive to competitive, entertaining Test cricket.

ICC advisors should be encouraged to be more critical of flat pitches. It would be preferable to find some way to reward groundsmen who prepare lively, challenging wickets, but it is difficult to imagine an incentive that could override a word in the ear from the chief executive. So, it is time to turn up the heat on turgid, boring pitches and hope that the number of bouncier tracks rises as a consequence.

Hand the Decision Review System (DRS) over to the umpires. There are lots of unintended, positive consequences to the DRS, such as the increased utility of left-arm spinners as attacking bowlers. But the DRS has also become a tactical tool, rather than a piece of technology to ensure the validity of decision-making. Giving teams unlimited reviews would cause the game to grind to an interminable halt, but nor is it fair that a batsman who is out can remain in because a team has used up its two appeals. By giving control of the DRS to the umpires, their continuing role in the game of cricket is preserved and it can be used when they believe it is necessary.

Find cricket's Bob Bowman. There is now sufficient interest in the digital-rights market that, if cricket is going to make the most of its biggest new revenue stream since the opening up of the Indian telecoms sector, a prototype of Major League Baseball Advanced Media's (MLBAM) AtBat needs to be drawn up soon. It will not be long before the England and Wales Cricket Board (ECB) or Cricket Australia (CA) attempts its own digital-only coverage, and it will only be a fraction as good as a global offering could be. But it will need a visionary to make it happen.

Grant the IPL a window in the Future Tours Programme, and then leave the fixtures calendar alone. The current iteration of the FTP is cluttered with short tours, and too many long series of one-day internationals (ODIs), but recent moves to change it, such as Sri Lanka's replacement of a Test series against South Africa in July-August 2013 with ODIs and T20 matches, are only making it worse.

Play the first-ever World Test Championship in 2017. Yes, it is artificial, and yes, it could crown a fairly undeserving team as the best in the world, but it is worth a go. When a Test series is played over four or five matches, its length justifies its existence. It becomes worth winning because so much time and energy has been spent on it. This is not the case with the increasing number of short tours, which feel perfunctory. A renewed emphasis on longer tours between the biggest nations and a short tournament, where the first and fourth-ranked teams and the second and third-ranked teams play a one-off Test, before another between the winners, would add a greater sense of purpose to the calendar. And, if it doesn't work, another idea will come along.

These suggestions would not appease all of those in the conservative or the liberal camps. The former would complain about the official approval of the IPL, the latter about the reform of the DRS. But, by taking the wisdom from both sides, accepting that cricket is a commercial enterprise, and also that it works best in some sort of context, more matches will be as exciting, as tough and as visceral as Newlands 2010. And if half of the games are as good as that, there will be no more need to talk about saving the Test.

Saving The Test
Acknowledgements

Acknowledgements

....

This book would not have been possible without the willingness of people from all over the cricket world to speak to me and answer my questions. More than anything, my faith in the future of cricket has been strengthened by talking to so many progressive and intelligent people who are passionate and committed to the sport. I would like to thank everybody that agreed to be interviewed, on or off record.

There are a few people that who ought to see their name in print. Alex and Hugo Loudon were immensely helpful at the time when I needed it most. Samanth Subramanian's generosity with his contacts book exceeded all expectations. Dileep Premachandran's responses to my frequent and pestering emails were much appreciated for a man with so little time. Sam Collins was a regular source of encouragement and enthusiasm and his film on Test cricket will be well worth a watch. My final chapter leant heavily on a superb article written by Chuck Salter, and was inspired by the mind of Stefan Szymanski. It was a delight to have one of my favourite writers on cricket, Jon Hotten, introduce this book. Tom Scruton and Rob Hardy were diligent and patient when correcting my numerous mistakes and clunky sentences.

As part of the research I was able to enjoy hours in the company of Malcolm and Lillian Knox in Sydney, Gideon Haigh in Melbourne, Johnny Barclay in Arundel, Peter Willey in Northampton and Ed Smith in London. There is no better way to learn about cricket than to play it, which is why the time I have spent with Neil Prothero, Sam Fox, Phil Whyte, Bill Ridgers, Duncan West, Graham Fowles and the rest of the Red Square Lions CC has been so special. Personal thanks go to Charlie Heald, Sujatha Santhanakrishnan, Sam Schwab, Josh Spero and Matthias Williams, and also to Keith and David Hartrick, for taking a punt on a rank outsider. My biggest debt of gratitude is to my fiancée, Amy. Despite my tendency to get utterly immersed in the game, she gave me total support and lots of self-belief (as well as plenty of eye-rolling). Without her I would never have had the confidence to write the first chapter. Thank you.

All errors are mine alone.

Saving The Test
Bibliography

Books

....

Atherton, M., *Opening Up: My Autobiography*, Hodder, 2003; *Gambling*, Hodder, 2006; *Glorious Summers and Discontents*, Simon & Schuster, 2011.

Bhattacharya, R., *Pundits from Pakistan*, Picador, 2005.

Bird, D., *My Autobiography*, Hodder, 1998.

Birley, D., *A Social History of English Cricket*, Aurum, 2003.

Blunden, E., *Cricket Country*, Pavilion, 1985.

Brearley, M., *The Art of Captaincy*, Pan Macmillan, 2001.

Buckland, W., *Pommies*, Matador, 2008.

Cowan, E., *In the Firing Line – Diary of a Season*, NewSouth, 2011.

Fraser, D., *Cricket and the Law*, Routledge, 2005.

Frith, D., *Frith on Cricket*, Great Northern Books, 2010.

Haigh, G., *The Green and Golden Age*, Aurum, 2008; *Inside Out*, Aurum, 2009; *Sphere of Influence*, Simon & Schuster, 2011.

Hamilton, Duncan., *Harold Larwood*, Quercus, 2009; *A Last English Summer*, Quercus, 2010.

Hawkins, E., *Bookie, Gambler, Fixer, Spy*, Bloomsbury, 2012.

James, C. L. R., *Beyond a Boundary*, Yellow Jersey Press, 2005.

Major, J., *More Than a Game*, Harper Perennial, 2007.

Martin-Jenkins, C., *The Spirit of Cricket*, Faber & Faber, 2004; *CMJ – A Cricketing Life*, Simon & Schuster, 2013.

McLean, T., *The Men in White Coats*, Hutchinson, 1987.

McLellan, A. (ed), *Nothing Sacred*, Two Heads, 1996.

Pycroft, J., *The Cricket-Field*, Nabu Press, 2010.

Rajan, A., *Twirlymen*, Yellow Jersey Press, 2011.

Szymanski, S., *Playbooks and Checkbooks*, Princeton University Press, 2009.

Wisden, various editions.

Wright, G., *Betrayal*, H. F. & G. Witherby, 1993.

Wright, J., *Indian Summers*, Souvenir Press, 2007.

Articles

....

Alderson, A., Leggat, D., Cleaver, D., 'Sport that lost its way from boardroom table to fans', *The New Zealand Herald*, 3 December 2012; 'Cricket and the media – a romance that went sour', *The New Zealand Herald*, 3 December 2012; 'All agree NZ cricket system broken, but where to next?', *The New Zealand Herald*, 3 December 2012.

Atherton, M., 'How reviews put players on their best behaviour', *The Times*, 21 June 2012.

Badel, P., 'South African allrounder Jacques Kallis attacks Twenty20 for destroying Test cricket', *Daily Telegraph*, 8 November 2011.

Bal, S., 'Learn the lessons of failure', *ESPNcricinfo*, 24 August 2011.

Baynes, D., 'International Cricket Council postpones World Test Championship until 2017', *Bloomberg*, 15 November 2011.

Berry, S., 'The ICC doesn't need a World Test Championship, just proper scheduling', *The Telegraph*, 17 Jul 2010; 'Cricket's iceberg beneath surface would be better detected if ICC adopted 'unexplained wealth' concept, *The Telegraph*, 5 November 2011.

Bhatia, R., 'Mr Big Deal', *Tehelka*, 20 May 2006.

Bhogle, H., 'Good enough for T20, good enough for Tests', *ESPNcricinfo*, 2 December 2011; 'India's system needs overhauling, not tweaking', *ESPNcricinfo*, 27 January 2012.

Bierley, S., 'Searching for young spin rebels – Ashley Giles need not apply', *The Guardian*, 18 May 2004.

Brearley, M., 'Pakistan cricket scandal: all too easy the descent into hell', The Guardian, 5 November 2011.

Brenkley, S., 'Paul Collingwood: Block and Awe', *The Independent*, 13 January 2010.

Brettig, D., 'Galle dustbowl rated 'poor' by ICC', *ESPNcricinfo*, 5 September 2011.

Bull, A. and Smyth, R., 'England v India – day two as it happened!', *The Guardian*, 11 August 2011.

Catone, J., 'Baseball Everywhere: How MLB is Innovating with Digital Media', *Mashable*, 26 August 2011.

Chopra, A., 'India, look after your young', *ESPNcricinfo*, 1 August 2012; 'U-19's fine, but don't forget first-class cricket', *ESPNcricinfo*, 10 August 2012.

Coverdale, B., 'Where have all the batsmen gone?', *ESPNcricinfo*, 6 November 2012.

Cowan, E., 'Why Australia needs spicy pitches', *ESPNcricinfo*,
15 September 2011; 'A real test? Not in your backyard', *ESPNcricinfo*,
7 June 2012.

Das, N., 'Indian Problem League: The sheen is wearing off',
Hindustan Times, 6 September 2012.

Dobell, G., "DRS has affected the game more than we thought it
would", *ESPNcricinfo*, 14 February 2012; 'Pietersen faces up to
DRS challenge', *ESPNcricinfo*, 17 February 2012; 'IPL 'catalyst'
in Pietersen controversy – Flower', *ESPNcricinfo*, 21 August 2012.

Dravid, R., 'The Bradman Oration 2011', *ESPNcricinfo*,
14 December 2011.

Edwards, RDJ., 'Tip off which triggered scandal came from
Pakistan camp', *ESPNcricinfo*, 2 November 2011; 'Lord Condon:
the full interview', *The Cricketer*, 18 November 2011.

Engineer, T., 'Star TV bags rights for Indian cricket',
ESPNcricinfo, 2 April 2012.

ESPNcricinfo staff, 'Pointing slams disappointing pitch',
ESPNcricinfo, 5 November 2004; 'SLC gets official warning
for Galle pitch', *ESPNcricinfo*, 7 October 2011.

Gollapudi, N., "The on-field umpire is in the best position",
ESPNcricinfo, 27 May 2008; "The ICC isn't trying to standardise
pitches', *ESPNcricinfo*, 3 August 2009; 'ICC suggests DRS policy
change, BCCI resists', *ESPNcricinfo*, 10 January 2013.

Haigh, G., 'What should the ICC be?', *ESPNcricinfo*,
27 September 2011.

Hansell, S., 'NBC's Olympic Web Blackout: The View from CBS and
Major League Baseball', *The New York Times*, 18 August 2008.

Hopps, D., 'The case for an IPL window', *ESPNcricinfo*, 31 May 2012; 'Magazine interview rebounds on Pietersen', *ESPNcricinfo*, 30 August 2012.

Hotten, J., 'Do Umpire Dream of Electric Sheep?', *The Old Batsman*, 6 April 2012; 'Chris Gayle: Grace, Bradman', *The Old Batsman*, 18 May 2012.

Hoult, N., 'Centurion 2000: Hussain still bitter about the day Cronje cheated', *The Telegraph*, 16 December 2004; 'International Cricket Council failed to follow tip-off due to lack of resources', *The Telegraph*, 3 November 2011.

Hughes, S., 'RP Singh is not fit to be Zaheer Khan's replacement', *The Telegraph*, 19 August 2011

John, E., 'Heads we lose', *The Observer*, 29 October 2006.

Lee, A., 'Umpire's decision is no longer final', *The Times*, 6 January 1996.

Lemon, G., 'Was the Sydney Test rigged?', *The Roar*, 7 September 2010.

Magazine, P., 'Not surprised, it was a disaster waiting to happen', *The Hindustan Times*, 14 August 2011.

Manthorp, N., 'Test series downgrade 'not ideal'', *Mail & Guardian*, 4 November 2011.

Marqusee, M., 'Privatisation and cricket: the Indian Premier League implodes', *Frontline*, 8 May 2010.

Marks, V., 'Virender Sehwag's magic touch can win a series but it may be too late', *The Guardian*, 9 August 2011.

Marsh, R., 'Summer of 242', *ESPNcricinfo*, 8 September 2011.

Martin-Jenkins, C., 'Why breaking the law is no sin', *The Times*, 19 January 2000; 'England triumph in game of forfeit', *The Times*, 19 January 2000.

Miller, A., "You'll never entirely eradicate fixing", *ESPNcricinfo*, 7 July 2010; 'ACSU head Ronnie Flanagan defends ICC', *ESPNcricinfo*, 3 September 2010.

Monga, S., 'Flat tracks make for pointless cricket', *ESPNcricinfo*, 30 July 2010; 'Curator defends SSC pitch for second Test', *ESPNcricinfo*, 31 July 2010.

Moonda, F., 'South Africa replace Boxing Day Test with T20', *ESPNcricinfo*, 5 June 2012; 'CSA hopeful of free-to-air broadcast', *ESPNcricinfo*, 17 December 2012.

Naidu, A., 'Indian tracks are no more spinner friendly: Bhajji', *The Times of India*, 18 November 2010.

Phillips, B., 'Soccer's New Match-Fixing Scandal', *Grantland*, 7 February 2013.

Premachandran, D., 'Chancy but vital', *ESPNcricinfo*, 15 October 2004; 'Of pitches and prejudice', *ESPNcricinfo*, 27 December 2005; 'Uniformity is for automatons', *ESPNcricinfo*, 11 May 2006; 'Those crying foul over The Oval pitch would do well to look at the facts', *The Guardian*, 26 August 2009; 'Are placid pitches to blame as Indian run Sri Lanka ragged?', *The Guardian*, 25 November 2009; 'In quest of a perfect itinerary', *ESPNcricinfo*, 23 August 2010; 'Why does Raina fail?', *ESPNcricinfo*, 20 September 2011; 'Test Championship is a sham', *Wisden India*, 22 March 2013.

Purohit, A., 'Raina seeks promotion to boost Test chances', *ESPNcricinfo*, 30 July 2012.

Reuters staff, 'ICC warns Indian board over 'poor' pitch in Kanpur', *Reuters*, 9 May 2008.

Roebuck, P., 'The enduring charm of Test cricket', *ESPNcricinfo*, 11 August 2010; 'All hail juicy pitches', *ESPNcricinfo*, 22 December 2010; 'Go back to the basics', *ESPNcricinfo*, 2 February 2011.

Ronay, B., 'Graeme Swann's absence gives England taste of how much he will be missed', *The Guardian,* 15 March 2013.

Salter, C., 'MLB Advanced Media's Bob Bowman is Playing Digital Hardball. And He's Winning.', *Fast Company*, 19 March 2012.

Scott, M., 'How the Pakistan three fell into a trap', *The Guardian*, 1 November 2011.

Selvey, M., 'A single Test, a century for two', *The Guardian*, 31 July 2000; 'ICC decision to stall Test championship threatens future of long game', *The Guardian*, 12 October 2011; 'DRS is a friend to nobody – for the good of the game it needs a rethink', *The Guardian*, 4 February 2012.

Smith, E., 'The problem's not Test cricket, it's bad Test cricket', *ESPNcricinfo*, 2 February 2012; 'What will the BCCI do with all its power?', *ESPNcricinfo*, 7 November 2012.

Stern, J., 'Doubts remain about Zaheer Khan as India's woes continue at Northants', *The Guardian*, 6 August 2011.

Subramanian, S., 'The Confidence Man', *Caravan*, 1 March 2011.

Szymanski, S., and Preston, I., 'Cheating in Contests', *Oxford Review of Economic Policy*, Vol. 19, No.4, 2003.

Ugra, S., 'T20: The future is here', *India Today*, 28 September 2007; 'Too much or too badly scheduled?, *ESPNcricinfo*, 19 August 2010; 'ICC defers decision on presidency', *ESPNcricinfo*, 29 June 2011, 'The IPL earns its street cred', *ESPNcricinfo*, 28 May 2012.

Vaughan, M., 'Pakistani convictions cast doubt over matches I played in – including Karachi', *The Telegraph*, 2 November 2011.

Wilde, S., 'Why we should all rejoice in bowlers having a ball', *The Sunday Times*, 25 December 2011.

Williams, R., 'Cricket and the lure of money – a sad tale with a long history', *The Guardian*, 29 August 2010.

Williamson, M., 'An offer too good to be true', *ESPNcricinfo*, 28 October 2006; 'Crash, bang and Pandora's box is opened', *ESPNcricinfo*, 25 August 2012.

Reports

. . . .

Argus, D., 'Australian Team Performance Review', 2011.

Central Bureau of Investigation, New Delhi, 'Report on Cricket Match Fixing and Related Malpractises', 2000.

Condon, P., 'Report on Corruption in International Cricket', 2001.

King, E. L., 'Commission of Inquiry into Cricket Match Fixing and Related Matters', 2001.

Qayyum, M. M., 'Cricket Inquiry Report', 2000.

Schofield, K., 'England Cricket Review', 2007.

Woolf, H., 'An independent governance review of the International Cricket Council', 2012.

Saving The Test
Index